T0286872

Comments about Jimmy Walker and
Walking by Faith, Serving in Love

"Jimmy is a true servant leader! His focus is always on helping others, and you will find in this book many stories about the importance of serving, which you will enjoy reading."

—**KEN BLANCHARD**, coauthor
of *The One Minute Manager*

"Jimmy is many things: generosity, solidarity, friendship. Everyone needs more faith, which is why I know Jimmy's book *Walking by Faith* will help many people."

— **ANDREA BOCELLI**, Italian
tenor and multi-instrumentalist

"Jimmy is one of my closest friends. Jimmy started a program for children from the inner city called Bicycles for Kids where they've given away ten thousand bicycles to children in need during the Christmas season. *Walking by Faith* can challenge all of us to give more by serving."

—**JERRY COLANGELO**, former
owner of the Phoenix Suns and Arizona
Diamondbacks and chairman the Naismith
Memorial Basketball Hall of Fame

"Jimmy Walker is my Christian brother who I have known for many years. Jimmy talks the talk and walks the walk with his faith. He provides refuge for addicts, giving them faith messages of hope and redemption with his Grace Sober Living homes."

—**ALICE COOPER**, Grammy-
nominated godfather of shock rock

"When I played on Jimmy's Phoenix Racquets team in World Team Tennis, you played matches, and then Jimmy would invite you to his Bible study."

—CHRIS EVERT, former world #1 tennis player

"The mold was definitely broken after God made Jimmy. He is one of a kind, a superhuman, a beautiful friend. *Walking by Faith* is a must-read."

—DAVID FOSTER, sixteen-time
Grammy Award–winning musician

"I first met the Walkers years ago when Nancy cosponsored an outreach in Phoenix and invited me to present the gospel. I was thoroughly blessed by her beautiful boldness to share God's love with her friends. Over the years, we have developed a lasting friendship that includes her husband, Jimmy. They have encouraged and inspired me by their words and example as I have witnessed them 'walking by faith' through the good times and the bad."

—ANNE GRAHAM LOTZ, bestselling
author and international speaker

"*Walking by Faith, Serving in Love* is the second wind we all need right now. Among the countless celebrities, pro athletes, and world leaders Jimmy Walker knows, here he reveals why his relationship with Jesus is the one he values most. With the warmth, wisdom, and winsome charm for which Jimmy's known, this book inspires us by example and challenges us by conviction."

—CHRIS HODGES, senior pastor
of Church of the Highlands

"I have so much respect for my friend Jimmy as a person, father, and husband. Please read *Walking by Faith, Serving in Love*."

—**LOU HOLTZ,** former University
of Notre Dame football coach

"Jimmy has a beautiful faith walk with God. When you read this book, it will help focus and expand your faith. When I read Jimmy's books, I'm lifted. Get ready to rise!"

—**JOHN MAXWELL,** bestselling
author and professional speaker

"I know Jimmy's book *Walking by Faith* is going to inspire so many people, just like Jimmy's faith has inspired me."

—**REBA MCENTIRE,** award-winning
country music artist, songwriter, and actress

"Jimmy is God's message on steroids. How can one man have so many projects on his plate and still have time for his own private life? The answer: Passion."

—**LIONEL RICHIE,** Grammy Award—winning
singer, songwriter, producer, and actor

"Jimmy has a hunger to lead people to Christ, and he does it in a very gentle and respectful way. The way he shares the gospel through living a life of service is inspiring. He is not ashamed to share the gospel with anyone. I know this book is going to make an impact on anyone who opens its pages. I am honored to call him friend."

—**MICHAEL W. SMITH,** Grammy
Award—winning singer and songwriter

"Jimmy's life is an inspiration. His example of faith in the face of great loss with his son, Scott, is a gift, and this book will encourage you."

—**RITA WILSON,** actress, singer, and producer

"Jimmy Walker is as comfortable speaking with the rich, the powerful, and the famous as he is with the homeless men and women who come to St. Vincent de Paul. This book should be read by everybody."

—**STEVE ZABILSKI,** former CEO of the Society of St. Vincent de Paul

"Jimmy Walker is one of those rare souls who meets you exactly where you are while making you feel like you're the only person in the room. The first time I met him, he treated me as if I had known him my entire life. Jimmy is the epitome of what it means to have a servant's heart and walk in the footsteps of Christ. I'm honored to know him and grateful men like him exist in the world."

—**JONATHAN ROUMIE,** American actor known for *The Chosen* (TV Series)

WALKING BY
FAITH,
SERVING IN
LOVE

WALKING BY
FAITH,
SERVING IN
LOVE

**16 PRACTICES
FOR GROWING IN THE
GRACE OF GOD**

JIMMY WALKER
FOREWORD BY RICK WARREN

Forefront
BOOKS

Published by Forefront Books, Nashville, Tennessee.
Distributed by Simon & Schuster.

Library of Congress Control Number: 2024914886

Print ISBN: 978-1-63763-209-3
E-book ISBN: 978-1-63763-210-9

Cover Design by Bruce Gore, Gore Studio, Inc.
Interior Design by Bill Kersey, KerseyGraphics

Printed in the United States of America

DEDICATION

*I*n 1967, I married Nancy, the most amazing woman in the world. She is my best friend whom I love. "Kindness" could be my wife's first name! Nancy is selfless, always thinking of others first—a result of her being humble and thoughtful.

Nancy's first love after Jesus is her family and me, along with our daughters: Laurie, Jennifer, and Cynthia Faye, who passed away six days after birth; and our son, Scott, who sadly overdosed on drugs at age forty-three. Nancy adores her seven grandchildren: Jack, Max, Macy, Jonathan, Mabel, Justin, and Kennedy.

There is a scripture that fits Nancy like a glove: "If you can find a truly good wife, she is worth more than precious gems" (Proverbs 31:10 TLB).

This book is dedicated to my "truly good wife," who is indeed precious.

CONTENTS

JIMMY WALKER:
A PURPOSE DRIVEN GUY

*I*n my fifty-plus years in the ministry, I've met a lot of impressive people. Presidents. Heads of state. Captains of industry. Fellow pastors and authors. And more than my fair share of celebrities. Among these standouts is a man in Arizona who most likely hasn't been on your radar but is doing big things nonetheless—my friend Jimmy Walker.

Jimmy Walker might not be a household name, but he has a Rolodex that can reach just about anyone in the United States, including presidents, billionaires, business tycoons, and plenty of A-list movie stars, professional athletes, and musicians. In a lengthy story in *Newsweek*, the magazine labeled him as "the man who schmoozed the world." Sure, Jimmy is a schmoozer (and a fine one, I might add), but his intentions have always been pure. Whatever Jimmy chooses to do, it's for the benefit of his fellow man. With the help of his vast network of friends, Jimmy has distributed approximately $100 million to various charities through Celebrity Fight Night, a nonprofit partnering with Muhammad Ali to raise money for Parkinson's disease research with the lead beneficiary being the Muhammad Ali Parkinson Center in Phoenix. Everyone comes out a winner when they associate with Jimmy.

I first met Jimmy on February 27, 2020, when he and Jerry Colangelo hosted a luncheon for me at the Arizona Biltmore in Phoenix. Michael W. Smith performed several songs prior to my talk, "Hope in Tough Times." It was a first-class affair with about five hundred people in attendance, and about a month before COVID-19 crippled the world.

When Jimmy met me at the airport, I gave him a great big hug. I felt we were instant brothers in Christ. But the hug wasn't for that reason. It was because Jimmy's son, Scott, had accidentally overdosed a few months before on December 12, 2019. Even though Jimmy was happy to see me, and we came together for a happy occasion, I recognized his pain and suffering. I knew it because a few years earlier, my twenty-seven-year-old son Matthew had taken his life after a lifelong battle with mental illness.

Naturally, Jimmy and his wife, Nancy, were still in deep grief over their loss of Scott. During my time with them, I shared how Jesus grieved the loss of Lazarus and that the grieving process is important. I have found through my ministry that many people stuff their sadness under a pillow only to have it resurface in other ways later, often with greater force.

I am thankful to have had the opportunity to spend that time ministering to the Walkers because it brought us that much closer. And through Jimmy's fine Christian example, he ministers to me in return through day-to-day life. I know many people on fire for the Lord, but Jimmy is in a different league: he's an unquenchable flame for Christ. He is an inexhaustible witness to everyone he encounters, never missing an opportunity to share the love of Jesus, such as the large backyard dinner parties he and his wife have hosted through the years where they invite a Christian with a platform to share his or her testimony before the meal is served. Almost every day Jimmy gives away McDonald's gift cards to the homeless in exchange for a moment of their time, telling them that God loves them. And once he even witnessed to a Muslim woman from India regarding a credit card issue. By the time they finished speaking, she had prayed with Jimmy to receive Christ. He is the greatest publicist the message of Christ could hope for.

Jimmy's latest mission is raising money for Grace Sober Living, in honor of his son, Scott. As of this writing, Jimmy and his family, along with their board, have developed seven Sober Living Homes and have several more in the works. These Christian-based sober living homes are nonprofit, which means they are being run properly and their motives are pure. Everyone involved, including many veterans of the recovery industry, say it's a first-class operation. I have no doubt because that's just how Jimmy rolls.

I could go on and on, singing Jimmy's praises, but I guess the purpose of this foreword is to set up this book you hold in your hands. The best thing I can say about *Walking by Faith* is that I have read it, digested it, pondered it, loved it, and highly recommend it. I am so inspired by Jimmy's testimony and lifelong Christian walk, because Jimmy inherently understands that true wealth comes from serving and making a difference in the lives of others and following the example of Jesus, our King of kings, who chose to be a servant rather than an earthly king. Proverbs 19:17 states, "Whoever is kind to the poor lends to the LORD, and he will reward them for what they have done."

Jimmy Walker is the living, breathing example of a Purpose Driven Life. We would all do well to follow his lead. You can start by reading the pages that follow.

Rick Warren
Author of *The Purpose Driven Life*
Pastor of Saddleback Church

SIX WEEKS THAT CHANGED MY LIFE

I grew up in the small town of Carthage, Illinois, and lived a pretty typical life. My goal as a kid was to be a professional basketball player. My parents required all of us to go to church. It didn't matter what church we went to, as long as we attended somewhere. Having the freedom to choose, I decided in grade school to go to the church that offered me the most fun and had good-looking girls.

In high school my biggest priority was basketball. When I was fifteen, I attended a Christian camp in Colorado called Young Life because it gave me a chance to play basketball and meet girls. It did give me something else that summer—I prayed to invite Jesus into my life.

Still, basketball continued to be a driving force in my life, and I attended Arizona State University on a basketball scholarship . . . but please don't google my basketball stats. I was enjoying my life, playing basketball, and partying with my Sigma Alpha Epsilon fraternity buddies. I just wanted to have a good time, so when

I met some guys in an organization called Campus Crusade for Christ, I did not want any part of them. They were nice, but frankly, I thought they were too religious. At the time I didn't want anybody giving me a bunch of rules for how to live my life. I sometimes went to church, but not consistently. I was majoring in basketball and minoring in girls, maybe with a second minor in catching rays.

You might find it amazing, then, that I got married young—I was twenty-two and Nancy was nineteen. (I fell hard for her.) We had our first child two years later; Cynthia Faye was born hydrocephalic and died within six days. Her death put Nancy in severe depression, and she was hospitalized for six weeks. After Nancy came home, several friends invited her to attend a Bible study. I thought it was fine for her to go, but I didn't think it was for me. My business was good. I had just purchased a World Team Tennis franchise with Reggie Jackson known as the Phoenix Racquets; I had signed Chris Evert, who was the number-one women's tennis player in the world; and I was having press conferences with the media. I had no complaints; however, I didn't have much time for prayer or God.

Even so, I was really happy Nancy went to Bible study. What I liked about it was that I saw changes in her life. She was no longer depressed; I saw a new joy and purpose, a new happiness. To see my wife smiling again was worth everything to me. After about a year, I decided to check out this Bible study since I had seen so many positive changes in Nancy's life. When I arrived for the first time, it probably took me thirty minutes to get from my car to the front door because I was still battling my resistance to Bible study, seeing religion as a crutch or an excuse. I had agreed to go, but I didn't see how it could benefit me since I wasn't depressed and I did go to church most of the time. When I finally made it into the study, I noticed an honesty in the twenty or so attendees that

I'd never experienced before. They were opening up about their lives and sharing stories about themselves. There was nothing fake about this first Bible study I attended.

The leader, Larry Wright, told me, "Jimmy, check this Bible study out for about six weeks, and if it doesn't work, forget it." I decided to give it a try, knowing I could always quit.

Not only did I go to the Bible study for those six weeks, but I continued going for six straight *months*, and then I asked Larry if he would lead one in our home. I came to realize I was seeking the truth in my life, and I found it studying the Bible.

Larry led Bible study in our home for about a year, and I invited many of my friends to come. When Larry shared that he and his wife, Sue, were moving to another Bible study and we would need a new leader, no one volunteered and I thought, *Oh my gosh . . . this Bible study is going to end*. I raised my hand and said, "Larry, I will lead." Nancy was so surprised I volunteered that she practically fell off her chair. I didn't feel qualified to lead Bible study and told Larry about my concerns, but Larry said, "Jimmy, if you lead this Bible study, that's between you and God; but, if you lead it, you can't help but grow."

That was around fifty years ago, and I'm still leading Bible studies today, which is a continual blessing.

CHAPTER 1

WHY I NEED TO READ THE BIBLE

"The Bible is more up-to-date
than tomorrow's newspaper."

Norman Vincent Peale recalled visiting a friend in the hospital who'd had one leg amputated and was about to lose the other leg. Peale said to him, "Everyone says you're the happiest person in the hospital. Are you putting everyone on?"

"No, I am as happy as I can be," the patient replied.

"Then let me know your secret," Peale said.

His friend pointed to the Bible in his hospital room. "See that Book over there? That is where I get my medicine. When I feel low, I just turn to the Book."

That could be my testimony as well. For so long the Word of God has brought peace, joy, guidance, and wisdom to my life.

The same is true for Zig Ziglar. Famous for his speaking and his impactful books on personal development and success, Zig was also a Christian who went home with the Lord at age eighty-six. Zig and his wife, Jean, for over twenty-five years purchased a bicycle for our Phoenix Bicycle Party for inner-city children, which our family has held during the Christmas season since 1984. To date, we have given away approximately ten thousand bicycles with our friends. Each child also receives a children's Bible in English or Spanish, along with their bicycle, helmet, and lock.

"For the word of God is alive and active. Sharper than any double-edged sword, it ... judges the thoughts and attitudes of the heart." — Hebrews 4:12

Zig's motivation was anchored in "the Book." He said, "I read the Bible every day and the newspaper every day. I read the Bible daily so I know what God is up to, and I read the newspaper daily so I know what the world is up to!"

Zig's most famous quote was, "You were born to win, but to be a winner, you must plan to win, be prepared to win, and expect to win." He also believed in the scripture from 2 Timothy 3:16, "All scripture is God-breathed and is useful for teaching, rebuking, correcting and training in righteousness."

When it comes to political matters, I have friends on both sides of the aisle. Many times I might say I'm not for the left wing or the right wing; I'm for the whole bird—I'm for America!

I've known Donald Trump long before he became president of the United States in 2017. I had often called and witnessed to him about the Lord. I still have a letter from him from December 29, 2009, thanking me for sending him a Bible.

In 2012 I called my friend and client Billy Crystal and asked if he thought it would be a good idea to honor Donald Trump at Celebrity Fight Night, a charity event I'd started in 1994 with Charles Barkley. Since Donald was a popular celebrity with his television show, *The Apprentice*, which ran for fourteen seasons, I knew his presence would help us to raise money. I knew Billy and Donald were both Yankees fans, and I thought it was natural to contact Billy first for his thoughts. Billy agreed and called Donald.

Sure enough, Donald agreed to attend. He sat next to Nancy at the charity dinner and they had an enjoyable visit. He stayed the entire evening and walked around the room, having his picture taken with many of our guests.

When Billy Crystal introduced Donald when he was receiving his award, he did a good job roasting him, mentioning Trump's airplane, Trump toilet paper, Trump soap, Trump paper clips, Trump hamburgers, Trump radios, and that he plays the Trump-et. We auctioned off a dinner with Donald at Jean George Restaurant in New York, and it went for a $350,000 donation to our charity.

When you read the Bible, you will read about the greatest man in history. His name is Jesus. He had no servants, yet they called Him Master. He had no degree, yet they called Him Teacher. He had no medicines, yet they called Him Healer. He had no army, yet kings feared Him. He won no military battles, yet He conquered the world. He committed no crime, yet they crucified Him. He was buried in a tomb, yet He lives today.

Billy Graham preached for fifty-eight years from the Bible to an estimated 215 million people who attended one or more of his four hundred crusades in more than 185 countries. Billy said, "Read the Bible carefully, thoughtfully, and prayerfully, asking God to help you understand it and apply it to your life. God will bless you through it."

I am an ordinary guy, imperfect and flawed. I don't consider myself better than anyone. I could make a list a mile long on woulda, coulda, shouldas! I have learned more from failing than from my successes. My life is littered with enough mistakes to fill this entire book. Walking by faith is not something I do perfectly, but I have a really important ally, the Holy Spirit, at my disposal who helps me navigate the road when I feel lost and don't know which way to go.

In the Christian life, sometimes we all need a reboot. There are times when I can't wait to read the Bible, when the anticipation of God's Word makes me want to shout with joy. But there are also times when I must rely on the words of my mentor, Larry Wright: "When you don't feel like reading the Bible, read it anyway." We can turn to the Bible as a way to get refreshed, especially if we're feeling cynical or exhausted. The Bible is very specific on how we can find spiritual refreshment for our souls in its words.

I asked my good friend Tom Shrader before he went home to be with the Lord, "What's your biggest challenge in being a Christian?" Tom said, "My answer is easy, I am too selfish." I told Tom I know *I* can be very selfish. We laughed about which of us could be more selfish.

"When I get up in the morning, I sit on the side of my bed and I say, 'God, if I don't get anything else done today, I want to know You more and love You better.'" — Rick Warren

---

The pace of modern life pulls us in many directions. We live in a world of distractions. But, realistically, it takes only eighty hours to read the entire Bible. With commitment and discipline, a person can easily read the Bible's sixty-six books in a calendar year.

Your Road Map: The Bible

My pastor at Scottsdale Bible Church, Jamie Rasmussen, frequently discusses how we tend to run *from* God instead of *to* God. We all fall into that category.

Too many people are looking for substitute religions and paths to contentment. Americans reportedly spend $30 billion a year on self-help programs, treatments, seminars, and a multitude of other things in an effort to find peace, hope, and tranquility in their lives.

By the time a typical American student graduates from high school, he or she will have spent more than thirty thousand hours in front of a screen. That's the equivalent of 1,250 days of video games, tablets, laptops, and televisions. The question becomes, "How are we choosing to spend our time?"

In today's world, it seems to be okay to be passionate about everything except God. We can be passionate about movies, sports, and the divisive realm of politics. We can be passionate about fashion, vanity, money, and our favorite restaurants. But if someone is overly passionate about their relationship with God, they are often criticized, if not shunned.

The Bible gives me all the guidance I need to take the right steps. It helps me know when I am off course and out of God's will. It gives me cautionary tales and inspiring stories as examples for how to live. But I had to learn how to use it effectively.

Before I became a Christian, trying to understand the Bible was like walking around with blinders on. It wasn't until the Holy

Spirit entered my heart, bringing me the truth and the meaning behind the Scripture, that those blinders came off.

And our enemies are always lurking in the shadows. They never sleep and never relent in trying to keep us from having a relationship with God. Satan doesn't mind if you attend Bible study, so long as those teachings disappear into the thin air and are never applied to your own life. Satan doesn't care what you know about the Bible, provided you don't do anything with that knowledge.

"The Bible will keep you from sin, or sin will keep you from the Bible." — Dwight L. Moody

---

For the rest of your life, you'll face great pressure to conform to the culture, and that probably means rejecting what God tells us in the Bible about how to live. This was Israel's biggest problem for thousands of years. They wanted to be like other nations. Yet God gave them all kinds of moral, civil, and ceremonial laws to make them different on purpose.

You may say, "I don't believe in the Bible."

If so, I want to ask you this: If you don't believe in the Bible, which has sold over five billion copies, what book do you believe in?

Many well-known Christians who have written hundreds of books on their faith—such as C. S. Lewis, Josh McDowell, and Lee Strobel—at one time did not place any faith in the Bible. They became believers when they took the time to read the Bible and allow it to speak to their hearts.

Throughout the Scriptures, we see lives transformed by God's Word. When Isaiah became close with God, he went from being depressed to standing courageously. When Paul finally met Jesus Christ, he was radically transformed from a persecutor of the faith to helping spread Christianity throughout the Roman world. And as Moses grew closer to God, he was transformed from the privileged son of Pharaoh to a humble servant leading God's people out of Egypt.

Jesus said the Bible will last until the end of time. It will accomplish everything God wants to do in this world. When Jesus talked about the Scriptures, He didn't read them as poetry or history. He saw them as something with a pulse and a heartbeat, something that changes lives.

And here is why *we* need to read the Bible: If we are fearful or anxious, there are countless Scriptures that will help us deal with fear and anxiousness. I am convinced that we do not have a problem for which God's Word doesn't have an answer.

What Is the Bible, and Why Should I Trust It?

The Bible is more than a book. It's a library of sixty-six books written by forty authors over a period of about fifteen hundred years. It was written on three different continents in three different languages. The thirty-nine books of the Old Testament were composed between 1400 and 400 BC, while the twenty-seven books of the New Testament were composed between AD 50 and AD 100. It is the most read, most published, and most translated book in the world.

The Bible is also much more than words. It is the most important book ever written. It stands above all other books. It guides. It teaches. It nourishes. It heals. It inspires. It saves. The Bible provides comfort and miracles and serves as your moral compass. It will give you everything you need in life and more.

The Bible brings us the living Word of God, which is omniscient, powerful, and authoritative. Either the Word of God is absolute, or it is obsolete. Develop a taste, and it is sweeter than honey dripping from a honeycomb. (See Psalm 19:10.)

The Word of God can change things you cannot change on your own. His words aren't just words on a page. They are filled with spirit and life. They are filled with redemption and salvation. God's Word can transform society and transform history. It can do the impossible. It can change your life.

"The Bible is alive, it speaks to me; it has feet, it runs after me; it has hands, it lays hold on me." — Martin Luther

---

The Bible gives us the truth. Without God's Word, you wouldn't be headed for heaven. You wouldn't know Jesus' death on the cross. You wouldn't know about God's purpose for your life.

God wants to give you all of these things, but it starts with His Word. Through the Bible, God recreates your life. When you feel like you're at the end of your rope, God uses the Bible to give you a fresh start, a do-over.

I understand that Bible study may sound daunting to you. If so, I recommend that you either join a Bible study group in which the Scripture is explained or find a pastor or Bible teacher who is very practical in their teaching and makes God's Word applicable to your everyday life.

Don't simply complain, "I try to read the Bible but I don't understand it." Be determined to find a way to understand it and begin by asking the Holy Spirit to help you learn something each time you open the Scripture to read it. After more than forty years

I still do that each morning when I study. The Holy Spirit is our Teacher. (See John 16:13.)

What is true of the church should be true of us as individuals. If you have no interest in the Bible, if you find it boring, then maybe you should ask yourself whether you know God as you really ought to.

To know the Bible is to know God. The Bible is God's love letter to you. No matter how lost and confused you might be, I know you will find that all of life's pressing questions are answered in the Bible.

"You were placed on earth to know God. Everything else is secondary." — Greg Laurie

---

How Do I Read the Bible?

I've learned from leading Bible study over the years that we need to possess a teachable spirit. Before we collectively open our Bibles, I encourage everyone in the room to be sure they are willing to go the distance in obeying God's Word. If God wants to speak to us, we need to be ready to listen, and we need to be ready to act.

It helps to declare your intentions and your faith when reading the Bible so you can hold yourself accountable. I remind myself to say the following words more often: "God, I'm willing to cooperate with whatever you want me to do. I'm signing a blank check. You fill in the amount!"

I have learned that I must constantly fight my selfish tendencies. I must sacrifice some of my busy time to make more room for God. I frequently notice my biggest excuse for not reading the Bible is that I'm too busy. But I have to admit that this excuse holds no water when I read Proverbs 10:27 (TLB): "Reverence for God adds hours to each day." It sounds impossible. But I can promise you it's true. The more time I spend with the Bible and in prayer, the more I seem to get things done. And trust me, you are never wasting time reading the Bible. That much I guarantee.

Make It a Habit

We all encounter dry spells when we are new in our faith. Don't allow anything to shake your commitment to prayer and to reading the Bible. It is important not to beat yourself up if you miss a day. Just understand the more often you skip, the harder it will be for you to stay committed.

Don't worry that you're doing something wrong if you don't have an emotional experience each time you open the Bible. The practice—the habit—is about replenishment, restoration, getting perspective and direction from the Lord. Reading the Bible daily is about filling your cup so you are equipped with the Lord's sustenance every day.

> **"All who have this hope in him purify themselves, just as he is pure."** — 1 John 3:3

Do you know anyone who eats well and exercises consistently? They may not always feel like eating vegetables and going to a health club after work, but they live by their commitments and their persistence pays off. They get where they are going in the end.

If you've ever read a Bible verse that seemed to jump off the page as if God were speaking directly to you—maybe it was an old verse that suddenly had new meaning or relevance—that's what having a daily practice can offer you. That's what it means to find refreshment from the Word of God.

Bottom line: The more we put God's words into practice, the more we become like Christ. And the more we vanquish evil.

Let It Fill Your Heart and Mind

We need to study and examine God's Word. It's the only way to protect ourselves from the counterfeit currency of Satan's lies. Reading the Bible fills your mind with God's perspective, which gives us the wisdom we need to lead a more fulfilling, productive life.

As we study Scripture, we are equipped for whatever comes our way. The truths and promises found in God's Word make their way into our hearts and lives, giving us strength to persevere in trials and courage to stand for Christ.

Reading and studying God's Word should be a priority, not a chore. God's words are life to us, and they bring healing to every area of our lives, including our inner lives. His Word is actually salve for a wounded soul. Just as there are different medicines available for various diseases and wounds, God's Word is medicine that heals our minds, emotions, wills, attitudes, consciences, and behaviors. It has a positive effect on our joy, peace, and confidence. It can cure fear, insecurity, and negativity.

Personally, I love memorizing Scripture. I feel it leads to a blessed life. I feel if I memorize Scripture, God's words are always with me, in my back pocket, on the tip of my tongue.

My mentor Larry Wright, who led the first Bible study in our home for Nancy and me, emphasized the importance of memorizing Scripture and then applying it in our lives. I still have scriptures taped on the wall in my bathroom to memorize today.

I've never studied the Bible without a pen and paper or an electronic device on hand. I love to take notes and highlight relevant passages. I try hard to understand how the Scripture applies to my life and what I might do with the accompanying clarity.

I read the Bible every morning, starting in the books of Psalms and Proverbs, because I'm searching for truth in this broken world.

"The Bible isn't to increase your knowledge; it is to change our lives." — Charles Spurgeon

---

James tells us that the key to a blessed life is to memorize Scripture—read it, review it, remember it, and respond to it—and it will bless your life. You may not think you have a good memory, but you remember what's important to you. You remember phone numbers and dates that you care about. You can quote songs from your childhood and rattle off the statistics of your favorite athletes. Memory is a skill you can learn. It's like a muscle you can strengthen with practice.

But it isn't enough just to know the Word of God in your mind. You have to know it in your heart as well. I've met people who have an impressive knowledge of the Bible; know Greek, Hebrew, and Aramaic; and have a vast knowledge of history. The problem is they're imbalanced. They have the knowledge. They have the doctrine. But they don't take those words to heart. They don't live with them and let them guide their steps each day.

There are also Christians who are lopsided in another way. They don't know much doctrinally or what the Bible teaches on certain subjects, but they're passionate about their faith in Jesus Christ. You might hear them say things like, "Let's not quibble over doctrine. I just love Jesus." Yet, if they're not careful, they might end up loving the wrong Jesus and believing the wrong gospel. That is where doctrine comes in. We need the balance of having both areas working together.

God wants us to have the wisdom of His viewpoint and evaluate everything according to biblical principles as we go through life. The Bible tells us that knowledge may be a prized commodity in the world, but what the Lord values is wisdom. (See Proverbs 8:11). So how do we gain wisdom? The first place to look is the Bible.

Use It to Overcome Obstacles

You will be tested as you read the Bible. You will come across words like *endurance* and *perseverance*. These words are often used when comparing the Christian life to a race or an athletic competition. You must deal with obstacles, fatigue, and crowds cheering for you to fail. You must remember the race is a marathon, not a sprint. You must pace yourself and preserve yourself. Most of all, you must finish the race, as Paul did: "I have fought the good fight, I have finished the race, I have kept the faith" (2 Timothy 4:7). And remember, nothing you face today is out of His reach, out of His control. The Bible is the road map teaching you how.

"The Bible is clear that God is in control of everything that happens." — Joni Eareckson Tada

---

From the world's perspective this does not seem reasonable; however, the truth is when we are getting clobbered with problems, we can cheer up and take courage if we are depending on the Lord to help us with our battle.

There is no better place to look for wisdom in this world than the Word of God. We can be looking for a new experience, truth, or revelation and get ourselves into a lot of trouble. Instead, we need to apply judgment and realize that we're potentially vulnerable. If we can't find it in the Bible, then we don't need it from someone else. The Bible is the arbiter of truth.

Jesus trusted the Scriptures—every word of them! He said that God's Word would last until the end of time and accomplish everything God wants to do in this world.

He would often base His arguments on a single sentence or even a single word. For Jesus, Scripture was (and is) the Word of God. He wants us to do more than read the Bible. He wants us to obey the Bible. Jesus wants us to trust the Scriptures just like He did.

No matter where you are on your spiritual journey, the Bible is your bridge, allowing you to get even closer to God, to experience real transformation in your life.

"The whole Bible was given to us by inspiration from God and is useful to teach us what is true and to make us realize what is wrong in our lives; it straightens us out and helps us do what is right." — 2 Timothy 3:16 TLB

As much as I love reading the Bible, it is also important to remember our fellowship is with God and not a book. The purpose of Scripture is to enable our fellowship with Him. The Bible is a living book that brings us into the presence of our living Savior.

You will also learn that Christianity is not for weaklings, wimps, or the faint of heart. It takes courageous men and women to follow Jesus, read their Bibles, and put His Word into action. So, it's okay to ask questions along the way. Children often ask questions on long road trips: "Are we there yet? How much longer? Why is it taking so long?" Children can't understand time, distance, delays, or detours. And we are like children before the glory of God, attempting to grasp His love, His grace, and His Word. It can be overwhelming, and questions are normal.

"God's laws are perfect. They protect us, make us wise, and give us joy and light." — Psalm 19:7 TLB

But at the end of the questioning, we still need to trust what God is telling us through His Word. Moses gave us the Ten Commandments in the book of Exodus. Sadly, too many people view the Ten Commandments as the Ten Suggestions. People can have their philosophy or opinions, but the Bible gives us the facts. I see an unfortunate trend in churches today where they disregard or marginalize the study of Scripture. If we do not study His Word, we will not be equipped when we face hardships or experience losses.

As a follower of Christ, you can expect that God sometimes will test your faith. And one of those tests comes when God's promises are delayed. What we often don't understand is that God has all of eternity to fulfill His promises. That means that some of His promises are not even going to be fulfilled until after your earthly life is over.

That's why God wants you to build your life on His promises. God is God, and you are not. He wants you to trust His promises, not wait for His explanations. After all, the Bible is full of promises, not explanations. There are over seven thousand promises of God in the Bible. They are designed to test and reward your faith, but He has not guaranteed that He'll fulfill every one of them instantly. God expects more from us. He wants more from us. But He is also very patient with us. And if you follow His Word, you will be rewarded in ways you cannot fathom.

Encouragement for Your Journey

Remember, God is always good. He is always trustworthy. The Bible is full of validation and prophecies that have always held true in the end. You must trust in the Word of God.

"God can't give us peace and happiness apart from Himself because there is no such thing." — C. S. Lewis

---

You will learn that being passionate about God delivers enormous awards. He will give His seekers true wisdom, joy, and a peace that transforms our life.

I want to share with you some of what I've learned along the way:

- I have learned if we abide by His Word we will know the truth, and the truth will set us free.
- I have learned the Word of God is living and active and sharper than any two-edged sword. Despise it and find yourself in trouble; obey it and you will succeed.
- I have learned every word of God is flawless.
- I have learned we are to be doers of the Bible and not just hearers.

- I have learned if you don't know the Scripture, you don't know the power of God.
- I have learned that, when I open the Bible, I feel God opening His mouth.
- I have learned that if we carry a Bible when we are young, it will carry us when we are older.
- I have learned the Bible is about transformation, not just information.
- I have learned that, in His eyes, we are all lovable, capable, valuable, forgivable, and usable.

God makes everything possible. He gives you wisdom and strength. He will fill your life with joy. How's that for comfort?

Let the Bible become the soundtrack of your life, and God will transform your mind. I discover a new truth every time I read it. I discover a new sense of joy every time I expose my mind to God's Word. That is how I know God is speaking to me.

Keep in mind, though, that it takes discipline to grow as a Christian. If you are not in the habit of reading the Bible, start off in small intervals, maybe five to ten minutes a day. You'll feel your appetite grow, along with your thirst for God's Word.

Most of all, I am in awe of His greatness. Despite those who ignore Him or rebel against Him, God loves every one of us. He proves it every day. He proved it beyond any doubt when He sent His Son, Jesus, to die on the cross for our sins. He loves us unconditionally, which is the very definition of *grace*.

When you memorize Bible verses, you always have God's Word with you. If you only keep your Bible on a desk at home, what good will it be when you're tempted at work, at the movies, in traffic, or at the grocery store? Memorizing Scripture gets the Bible off your desk and into your heart. Once it's in your heart, the Holy Spirit can bring it back to your mind in the moment of temptation, so you can replace the devil's ideas with the truth of God's Word.

"The great thing to remember is that though our feelings come and go, God's love for us does not." — C. S. Lewis

---

So, since you do have the time, the question is, "How will you use your time?" God's Word gives you the wisdom you need to live a fulfilling and productive life.

I like to keep these truths in mind as I go about my day: The Word of God is either absolute or obsolete. The Bible may hurt you with the truth, but it will never comfort you with a lie.

In fact, research shows that destructive habits decrease and positive habits increase when people are in God's Word at least four days a week. Someone who reads the Bible four or more times a week is

- 59 percent less likely to view pornography.
- 74 percent less likely to gamble.
- 228 percent more likely to share their faith with others.
- 231 percent more likely to disciple others.
- 407 percent more likely to memorize Scripture.

These same people are 30 percent less likely to struggle with loneliness.

I can get on a slippery path when I find myself too busy to pray or too busy to spend time in God's Word. I like the scripture, "For promotion and power come from nowhere on earth, but only from God" (Psalm 75:6 TLB). That's because when it comes right down to it, I believe in God, who is the God of miracles and who has awesome power.

As Billy Graham said, "Life without God is like an unsharpened pencil, it has no point."

I like what NFL superstar Russell Wilson said when receiving the Muhammad Ali Humanitarian Award at Celebrity Fight Night. He quoted John 3:30, "He must increase, but I must decrease."

Sizzling Steak—and Much More

To close this first chapter, let me tell you about a monthly event I hold with my four grandsons. We call it Papa's Steak Night. It's fifteen minutes of Bible study followed by fifteen minutes on the subject of hospitality. Then I cook a steak dinner. We read chapters from Rick Warren's book *The Purpose Driven Life*. The kids ask me great questions, and it's important that I make the Bible study fun.

When it comes to hospitality, I stress to my grandchildren the importance of the little things like opening a door for a woman, how to say "Sir" and "Ma'am," how to look a person in the eye and deliver a firm handshake, and how to say the words "Nice meeting you." (Unfortunately, hospitality classes tend not to be taught in school these days.)

I have been doing this for over a decade. When the kids were younger, they just giggled and devoured the steak. Now they are really paying attention. They have come to understand the importance of good manners, the power of saying "Thank you" and "You're welcome," and many other vital life tools and wisdom.

By the way, my grandson Justin said to me at the age of eight, "Papa, you are not very good with computers."

"I know that, Justin," I said, "but don't ever forget, Papa taught you the right way to use a spoon."

The Bible can do much more than teach us to be polite and give a firm handshake; God's Word can and will completely transform our lives if we let it—and that's why I need to read it every day.

CHAPTER 2

WHY I NEED TO PRAY

"They say seven days without
prayer makes one weak."

*C*hick-fil-A, Hobby Lobby, and In-N-Out Burger encourage their employees to pray and to read their Bibles. Chick-fil-A's chairman, Dan Cathy (son of founder, Truett Cathy), closes its restaurants on Sundays, hoping employees will use that time to attend church and spend time with their families. Chick-fil-A, which has over three thousand restaurants, wants their employees to glorify God by being faithful stewards of all that is entrusted to them.

In-N-Out Burger, which has more than four hundred restaurants (and is growing fast), puts Bible verses on its cups and wrappings.

Hobby Lobby, which has almost one thousand stores, believes in honoring the Lord. Their goal is to operate according to biblical principles.

Prayer is still a regular part of many Americans' lives. For example, the annual President's prayer breakfast, now known as the National Prayer Breakfast, is held every February in Washington, DC. Its purpose is to pray for our nation. The chaplain of the US House and Senate opens meetings of the legislative bodies with prayer.

Unfortunately, prayer has been taken out of the public schools, along with the Bible. Yet in prisons, prayer and the Bible are encouraged. Perhaps if we had more prayer and Bible teaching in our schools, we wouldn't have as many people in prison.

Before Tim Tebow, who was well known for kneeling in prayer before NFL games, many all-pro players like Reggie White and Mike Singletary years ago were kneeling to pray before and after games. Only a few adults disapprove when an athlete is seen praying on the field or expressing their faith publicly. However, some people were more upset when Tebow was praying even during games, while some of those same people thought it was okay for teammates to gather and pray when a player was injured, which sounds like a double standard. Romans 1:16 tells us we are not to be ashamed of the gospel, and the gospel makes it very clear that we are to be constantly in prayer.

Evangelist John Wesley used to say that he thought very little of a man who did not pray four hours every day. He would rise at 4:00 a.m. every day to seek God for the first four hours. In his later years, Wesley was known to spend up to *eight* hours in prayer daily. He was always looking for a word from the Lord.

Rock and roll icon Alice Cooper has a similar routine. This is what Cooper told *The Times UK*: "I'm up before the sun; 5:00 a.m. is my time. Straight out of bed, make a cup of coffee, grab my Bible, then spend the next hour reading and praying. I read a couple of chapters a day. It puts me in a positive frame of mind."

What Is Prayer?

Prayer is simply talking to God, and God wants us to talk to Him. He loves us and He hears our prayers. The Bible tells us that David prayed seven times a day. He fasted and prayed nonstop for three straight weeks. Jesus is shown to have prayed at least thirty-eight specific times in the Gospels. The Bible shares the Jesus would go into the high hills to spend the whole night in prayer.

Pray and believe and expect to receive. Pray and doubt and expect to be left out.

Does God always answer our prayers the way we might think is best? No, He doesn't, because His ways are higher and we don't always understand them at the time. When Garth Brooks sang at Celebrity Fight Night, I was always struck by his song "Unanswered Prayers." He sang, "Some of God's greatest gifts are unanswered prayers." And Ruth Graham once said that if God answered every one of her prayers, there were three other men she could have married instead of Billy Graham. (By the way, Billy himself once said, "All of my prayers were answered except when I was on the golf course!")

Is prayer required to be a formal exercise, scripted and sanitized? Not at all.

Did you know the microwave oven was discovered by accident in 1946, after a laboratory test melted an engineer's snack? Today, over 90 percent of homes feature a microwave oven. Few inventions better symbolize our hurry-up society and a culture that demands instant gratification.

Now, how does that relate to prayer? I use the idea of a microwave when it comes to my prayers throughout the day while I'm working or going about the responsibilities in my life. These are prayers that might be anywhere from thirty seconds to three minutes.

They are the kind I lift up to God when waiting in traffic or in line at the grocery store, and the person in front of me pulls out fifteen coupons and reviews each one with the cashier, leaving me to wait and wait to pay for my groceries. Microwave prayers are for the moments when you need immediate guidance—when you need to get right to the point—when you need to get God on the hotline ASAP.

Microwave prayers help in moments of extreme stress when your anger might get the best of you, or in moments of temptation, where you might do something you'll soon regret. They sometimes reflect immediate needs in key moments of our lives.

One time Kelly Clarkson performed at Celebrity Fight Night and was singing her heart out before a room full of a thousand-plus attendees. Suddenly she asked a few women to join her onstage. However, within sixty seconds over *one hundred* women had rushed to the stage. Remember, I'm an insurance guy, not a show-biz guy. I felt my heart quicken. I thought it was a bad idea because that stage wasn't designed to hold two hundred folks at once! People flooded the stage. I looked up and saw my wife dancing with Billy Crystal's wife, Janice. I could see the stage bending and buckling like a bridge during an earthquake. I said some microwave prayers that evening. And thankfully, the stage remained intact. God was listening, and against all odds, no one was hurt.

Regardless of how you pray or what you pray for, I hope you recognize the importance of prayer for building your relationship with God, because He will use those conversations to reveal the power of prayer in your life and in the lives of others.

On January 6, 2023, Buffalo Bills player Damar Hamlin was seriously injured and almost died on the field when the Bills were playing the Cincinnati Bengals. Hamlin's shocking collapse drove a nation to pray. All the players on both teams knelt in prayer on national television. Even the broadcast announcers were encouraging everyone to pray.

Hamlin's injury during *Monday Night Football*, along with an unprecedented outpouring of love, support, and even public prayer for the twenty-four-year-old, riveted the country. After all, when is the last time you saw a sports analyst, along with his colleagues on ESPN, bowing their heads and calling out to the Lord in prayer? America has never seen more media coverage about the importance of prayer than when Hamlin was hospitalized after experiencing cardiac arrest. And in his recovery, I believe we saw God answer prayer in real time. Prayer makes a difference.

Pastor and author Charles Stanley has said that God knows our future and wants to counsel us. For that reason it is foolish to make decisions without seeking God's wisdom by going to prayer, since He knows everything and He loves us unconditionally.

During my twenty-seven years organizing Celebrity Fight Night, the majority of those years working with Muhammad Ali, there were times when it felt like I was walking on a high wire without a safety net. I oversaw a ballroom full of superstar athletes and entertainers. I was faced with a lot of quick decisions with my planning, and many times I made decisions without praying first. That didn't always end well.

For example, one decision I regret involved Tom Brady, a seven-time Super Bowl champion who most consider the greatest quarterback in NFL history. Early in his career, I invited Brady to attend Celebrity Fight Night as my guest. While he was in Arizona, I put Tom together with my good friend Foster Friess to play golf at Estancia, my club in Scottsdale, which he very much appreciated. I introduced him to one of the biggest sporting icons of all-time, Muhammad Ali. Our relationship was off to a great start.

The following year, Brady wanted to return to Celebrity Fight Night, but this time he had a list of requirements, including event tickets, airfare, and hotel rooms for four friends. I told Tom that we were a charitable event with many expenses and could not include his friends.

If I had stopped to pray about my decision, I would have worked out some way for Tom to bring his friends. I would've told him to bring along his sisters, brothers, friends, cousins, cats, dogs—whomever and whatever he desired. I reacted rashly, and that cost me a friend and supporter. I never got Brady to return to Celebrity Fight Night.

My advice? When you're asked to do something that seems impossible, when you're placed in a very difficult situation, when you need to choose one of several viable options, put it first to prayer before making a quick decision.

Why Worry When You Can Pray?

Persistent prayer focuses our attention. When we pray over and over, it's not to remind God; He not only remembers what we asked for the first time, He knew what we were going to ask before we asked it. No, repeated prayers are to remind *us* that God is the source of every answer to the questions we face in life.

Persistent prayer also tests our faith. God is always working in our hearts to draw us closer to be more dependent on Him.

It took me a while to learn how much prayer could change my life, but now I turn to prayer for everything. I believe prayer is good for your soul and your health. One recent study tried to quantify the power of prayer and summarized that people who engaged in frequent prayer lived longer lives. Maybe it's because those who pray on a regular basis have a more positive outlook on life and know how to handle stress.

We should never question God's timing, because we don't understand everything that is involved in answering our prayer. Our role is to not be discouraged and to never give up. Even though you don't know why God hasn't answered your prayers, you can trust Him to keep His promise. It's fine to pray for a miracle, but don't be surprised if the result is gradual change. Rick Warren said if God answered every prayer immediately, you would begin to think He was nothing but a vending machine—insert a prayer, push a button, and whatever you need drops into the tray. Fortunately, that's not how it works.

Sometimes God will say no because what we are asking for is not in alignment with His plan for us or is not in our best interests. We can all fall into the trap of being selfish when we pray, and sometimes, just like when a child asks his parents for candy right before bed, the answer has to be no because what we want isn't good for us. When that happens, we need to thank God for not answering all of our prayers.

The objective of prayer is to praise God even though we may not understand what He is trying to do in our lives. And if we're willing to submit to His plans, we will position ourselves to be used greatly by Him. When the Lord blesses you, He's not only doing something for you; He's also doing something in and through you to affect others' lives.

I am at a point in my life where unless I pray first thing in the morning, I can't function properly. Make prayer time the best time of your day.

Think you're too busy to pray? Nonsense. The latest research shows most Americans check their social media accounts seventeen times a day. We binge-watch television series at a historic pace. Some of that time would be much better spent in prayer.

I strive to be in constant prayer. I spend most of my prayers expressing gratitude, saying thanks for everything, including the eternal life to come. But I also take my problems and concerns to the Lord. The more I pray, the more I have to say to God in prayer because it helps me see all the things in my life to be grateful for and helps me to lean on Him for everything. My prayer becomes persistent.

Sometimes I start my prayers by saying, "Lord, I know I am a mess in so many ways, but I know you are the message."

I might drift when I pray—daydreaming, even fantasizing—and in those moments, I try to lasso those thoughts and bring the conversation back to God.

How and When Should You Pray?

I am sure you have uttered a prayer under your breath in a moment of crisis or when you hoped for a good outcome in a situation. You may not have been fully aware of how prayer works or even who you were praying to, but we all have the impulse to reach out to someone or something beyond us when we need help.

"Prayer is the practice of drawing on the grace of God." — Oswald Chambers

---

God sent us a letter with all we need to know: the Bible. Our prayers are the letters we send to Him. And we can send them any time we want, no postage due! In fact, God's inbox is always open to us.

We tend to think of prayer as that poem we were taught to recite as children, when we were forced to kneel beside our beds before going to sleep, the blessing we say before a meal, the thing we whisper before we take that potentially game-winning shot on the court, or the plea we make when we fear we are in trouble.

Those are definitely times to pray, but they aren't the only ones. Prayers are not like multivitamins you take once a day to boost your performance. God wants to listen to and answer your prayers, but this misconception turns prayer into a trade where you beg, bribe, and bargain: "God, if You do this, I will do that." God doesn't want your prayer to resemble a transaction; instead, He wants to use it as a catalyst for transformation.

Prayer is not a ritual to relieve guilt. You don't need to say the same prayer over and over again to remove your guilt. Prayer is simply a conversation with God where you tell Him what's on your heart and then receive the mercy and grace that you need today. It is an ongoing dialogue—a chance to talk with God and get to know your heavenly Father, to tell Him what is going on inside your heart, to find the mercy and the grace you need. Sadly, most people underutilize the power of prayer in their lives. In fact, even most Christians don't really understand how to really pray and bring God into every moment of their day.

Why Should You Pray?

If you aren't a Christian and don't have a relationship with God, prayer is a great place to start connecting with Him and letting Him speak to your heart. If you are a Christian and you feel stuck in a situation or just want to have a deeper relationship with God, prayer is the key to unlocking the door to growth.

So, why should you pray? Let me ask you this: Do you find yourself needing more time, energy, knowledge, or opportunity? Well, prayer is a great place to start. Start by making this your daily prayer: "Lord, if I don't accomplish anything else today, I want to get to know You a little better. I want to love You a little bit more."

Praying for God to give us hearts that love, serve, and obey Him opens us to God's strength and guidance. It is only with a heart completely submitted to Him that we are able to live the life He calls us to live.

————

"There are many things that are essential to arriving at true peace of mind and one of the most important is faith, which cannot be acquired without prayer." — John Wooden

————

Prayer keeps you focused, tuned in. When you pray over and over again, it's not meant to remind God; it's meant to remind you that God is the source of your answer. If we only pray during set times each day or when we want Him to fix something, we miss out on the dynamic of praying without ceasing. You might think you can handle things on your own and that relying on God to solve everything for you makes you weak, but persistent prayer gives you access to the greatest source of strength. The more you pray, the more answers you'll receive.

Prayers can be silent and flow all day long, and you don't need fancy words to speak to God. You don't need a special website and password. You can speak to Him conversationally, about whatever you're interested in. It's not hard to make the switch from talking to yourself to talking with God, and the benefits are immense.

God is always listening, always ready to welcome His children into His presence. He takes pleasure in hearing our prayers. And I am constantly amazed at how I can go into prayer in a certain mood and come out in another mood altogether.

Prayer can give you the power to overcome any challenges in your life—disappointments from losses, disagreements with others, confusion about decisions you have to make, addictions or other health problems. Remember, God doesn't want us to run from the giants in our lives. He wants us to attack them. No matter the giant in your life, He will help you find the strength to confront it and do what you need to conquer it. Call on God and pray for His power.

You may feel weird praying at first. Many people are especially terrified of praying with others, and I don't blame them, but that's because they don't have a daily personal practice of it. If you will start by just trying to have a conversation with God while you are doing a household chore or sitting in traffic, eventually your prayers will become like breathing. They will happen organically, automatically. Prayer is to your soul what breathing is to your body.

On the days when you're unsure of how to pray, spend time thanking God for faith, family, friends, and finances. Praise and gratitude are the best ways to start a conversation with God.

"A true prayer is an inventory of needs, a catalog of necessities, an exposure of secret wounds." — Charles Spurgeon

---

Then tell God what you are feeling. Tell Him about your nervousness, anxiety, excitement, and frustrations. God already knows everything about you, but He wants to talk with you. He wants to hear from you.

Many times I have a supply of excuses because I don't take time to pray. Some days you may not feel like having a quiet time, but do it anyway. If you wait to have a quiet time until you feel like it, Satan will make sure you never feel like it.

I want to challenge you to develop the habit of spending daily time with Jesus. When you stay connected to Him, you'll find your life overflowing with God's goodness and power, and you'll realize that's all you really need.

How Prayer Works

We need to teach ourselves how to pray. We pray about the big things, but let's not forget about the little things. Small problems can become big issues, especially if we neglect them. When you pray before making a big decision, you are slowing down long enough to make a wise choice. In moments of unexpected stress, we need to turn our panic into prayer. We need to turn our worry into worship.

We are passionate in prayer whenever we need something from God, and there's nothing wrong with that. But after God has answered our prayers, we also have to make sure we are just as passionate about giving Him thanks. Remember to show gratitude for His faithfulness to us and pray with a heart full of thankfulness.

"Prayer is the Christian's most powerful God-given means for effecting change." — Charles Stanley

---

It's a good idea to pray like the psalmists did: "Search me, God, and know my heart.... See if there is any offensive way in me, and lead me in the way everlasting" (Psalm 139:23, 24).

Be specific with your requests and your gratitude. Instead of asking God, "Will You help me today?" say, "Help me to have a good attitude." Instead of saying, "Thank You for everything," tell God exactly what you are grateful for. Be specific.

I have found that God doesn't always speak to us right away during prayer time. When we go to the Lord in prayer, we must be willing to hear what He says, whether that's now or later. Too often, we don't stop to listen to Him. We must learn to wait for His voice to appear, in some form or another.

"God does not ignore our prayers." — See Psalm 9:12

He might end up speaking to you two days later, while you're doing something completely unrelated. That is why you must keep your heart and your ears open. That's also why learning how to stay in continual conversation is important. If you keep the channel of communication open with God, you are better able to hear when He speaks. But don't be discouraged when God's answers for your prayers don't come as quickly as you want; He is up to something good.

One of the most difficult aspects of prayer is perseverance. Too often, our newly made commitments to be more consistent fail, and one of the main reasons for this is if we think God isn't answering us. But God's promise to answer His children's prayers hasn't proven false—even if we don't see results as we hoped. Every prayer will be answered, but sometimes, God says "no"; sometimes, God says "slow"; and sometimes, God says "go."

If you pray repeatedly and think you're not getting an answer from God, you probably need to ask yourself if you have missed

His answer because it didn't come in the form you were expecting. If you received instant results every time you said a prayer, you would only focus on the blessing. God wants us to focus on the Blesser.

Jesus prayed, "Yet not as I will, but as you will" (Matthew 26:39). Ultimately, Jesus was committed to obeying the Father. Jesus offered a prayer of absolute surrender. You can be honest about your feelings with God. He knows them anyway! You also need to surrender your life to Him if you want His will to be done in your life.

"Do not be anxious about anything, but in every situation, by prayer and petition, with thanksgiving, present your requests to God." — Philippians 4:6–7

We also need to understand that God may be answering our prayers, but not as we ask. Sometimes He wants to give us the desires of our hearts, but the timetable we want isn't right. For instance, you might ask God to help you get out of debt, and He is pleased to help you with that, but He might want to build your character in the process, so He won't send you an immediate solution. He may want you to learn how to do that over time so you don't repeat the mistakes that got you there in the first place, or He may want you to build a solid foundation so you can avoid that situation in the future.

When we don't get the answers we expect, we might want to give up on prayer or even on the Lord Himself. God is delighted to answer the prayers of believers who earnestly seek His will. In the Sermon on the Mount, Jesus uses three verbs to describe prayer:

ask, *seek*, and *knock*. Prayer is more than merely making requests of God. It involves *asking* for Him to guide us and *seeking* His will.

We also must realize that there are things that can hinder our prayers. If we are burdened by sin or shame, we might not feel good about speaking with God, especially if we haven't confessed. Opening our hearts to God will remove those obstacles so we can have an audience with Him. That is one of the reasons starting with gratitude and praise is so important. Thanking God and acknowledging His greatness is a sure way to open your heart to Him.

As you begin to pray, and you understand how to manage your expectations, you also need to remember to be careful what you pray for. God is going to use the things we ask for to teach us and help us grow. If we pray for patience, we are likely to face interruptions, delays, and distractions that will test and stretch our ability to be patient. If we pray for generosity, we will likely encounter people or charities that could benefit from our resources. And if we pray for perseverance, there is a good chance we will begin experiencing trials and tribulations. In other words, character traits are developed only by situations that test those very traits in our daily lives.

"Consider it pure joy, my brothers and sisters, whenever you face trials of many kinds, because you know that the testing of your faith produces perseverance." — James 1:2–3

When James wrote his letter to believers who had been scattered abroad, he told them that the testing of their faith would produce patience. And that patience has a goal: our spiritual and emotional maturity. Immature people become discouraged easily. Therefore, we need experiences that will teach us not to become discouraged and will make us more mature.

Maturity is synonymous with Christlikeness. God uses everything in life—especially the hard things—to conform us to the image of Christ (Romans 8:28–29).

Maintaining your prayer life will help you to keep seeking God so you depend on Him for everything. Do you pray about your work or do you just jump in and do it? You ought to pray about everything God places before you. Ask God for wisdom and ask Him to bless it.

Encouragement: The Power of Prayer

Maybe you've never spent time with God, or maybe you have, but it's been weeks or months. That's why you're overloaded. You need to spend time alone with God in silence. As you sit with Him, spend time praying and reading the Bible.

I like to pray first thing in the morning. I believe we should all wake up and show our gratitude to God. We should thank Him for all that we have and not complain about what is missing in our lives. Then I read the Bible.

Persistent prayers prepare your heart for the answer. Sometimes God denies your prayer requests because you're thinking too small and asking too little. He wants to give you something better. But first, He has to prepare you for it.

If you've given up on praying persistently, today is the day to renew your commitment to pray specifically.

I pray when I feel inadequate, and I end up receiving my best ideas through God's divine guidance, whether the matters are personal or business-related. I spend much of my time in service to the Lord, so one of my prayers is for balance in my life because there is so little time available and so much good that needs to be done.

Consider your commitments very carefully and pray before taking action. God wants you to ponder before promising. You will reduce stress when you count the cost of committing to something new. Take time to pause and pray before saying yes.

The Bible tells us to pray all the time, but how can you do that? One way is to use "breath prayers" throughout the day, as many Christians have done for centuries. Choose a brief sentence or a simple phrase that can be repeated to Jesus in one breath: "You are with me." "I receive Your grace." "I'm depending on You." "I want to know You." "I belong to You." "Help me trust You."

Why should you be persistent in your prayers, even when you don't get an answer?

First, persistent prayers focus your attention. If every time you prayed you instantly got results, you'd only think about the blessing. God wants you to focus on the Blesser.

Second, persistent prayers clarify your request and refine what you are asking of Him. God wants to answer your prayers, but He wants to be certain it's what you really want. This process helps you to develop more wisdom.

Finally, persistent prayers test your faith. When God delays your answer, you are at a crossroads. Will you wait for Him to act, or will you take it upon yourself to come up with a solution? God is always working in our hearts to be more dependent on Him.

If you have given up on praying persistently and specifically, today is the day to renew your commitment.

You need to pray with an attitude of thankfulness. The way to pray is to be specific with your requests and your gratitude.

"Rejoice always, pray continually, give thanks in all circumstances; for this is God's will for you in Christ Jesus." — 1 Thessalonians 5:16–18

Prayer is not a magic wand or an instant fix that will change all of your circumstances. God loves you unconditionally, but He doesn't respond to your prayers with "Your wish is My command." We serve God, not the other way around.

It's easy to pray on the bad days—when you need help—but you also need to pray on the good days. Prayer isn't the last option after you have tried everything else: it ought to be your first choice. Prayer is a privilege, not a duty. Prayer ought to be joyful.

CHAPTER 3

WHY I AM OFTEN TEMPTED

"I am tempted to always want everyone to agree with me. After all, I am an easy guy to get along with as long as you agree with me."

Temptation is everywhere in this world. I feel it every day, and it begins in the mind. Sometimes I'm tempted to do things that are physically unhealthy like consume lots of calories or drive over the speed limit, and sometimes I'm tempted to do things that are emotionally or mentally unhealthy such as gossiping, being overly judgmental, or envying others.

When I was in college and on the basketball team at Arizona State, I was tempted to cheat on exams along with some of my friends. I was in the Sigma Alpha Epsilon fraternity, and some of my fraternity brothers were receiving final exam tests in advance.

I was told one of the football players (who was probably the best-looking guy on campus) was dating the professor's secretary. She was going to give the football player the test she was typing for her boss, and he would sell the test to some of the guys in our fraternity house. I took advantage of this offer and used the test to prepare, even though I knew I would be labeled a cheater. And after that decision, I found it became really easy to cheat again when I was told the professor who taught a very difficult engineering class would give the players on the basketball team a good grade if we just showed up in his class a couple of times.

This was a very difficult course, and the engineering professor loved athletes at Arizona State. I received a B by going to two classes—but I also felt lousy with guilt.

Many years ago Dr. Jerry Buss, one of the most flamboyant and successful owners in the history of professional sports, and I were business partners in World Team Tennis (WTT). He owned the Los Angeles franchise and I owned the Phoenix Racquets. He took an instant liking to me, even fronting me the $50,000 I needed to be seated at WTT league meetings.

Later in our relationship, Dr. Buss came to me with the idea of buying the Phoenix Playboy Club. He thought it would really be fun. And, frankly, I was tempted for about ten seconds, but then I said, "Jerry I don't think that would go over too well with Nancy, and besides that I lead a Bible study."

Jerry quickly replied, "Jimmy, you're right, this wouldn't be a good decision for you." I said, "Thanks anyway for asking."

As I said, it was tempting. And even though I had been a Christian for some time, I had to stop myself from entertaining an idea that would not lead to honoring my wife or being a good example to others.

I was also tempted in Toronto to judge Steven Tyler. I attended David Foster's charity event, where Tyler, the Aerosmith singer and television star, was the headline performer. Foster asked me to do an invocation before about fifteen hundred people. I thought, *Steven Tyler is probably the most disinterested person in this room when it comes to hearing me give an invocation.*

After the invocation, I received an incredible surprise. Steven was the first person to come up to me and compliment me on my prayer. The prayer wasn't the mistake; it was the judging. I had thought, *Steven Tyler, with his long hair and rock and roll attitude, couldn't care less about a prayer.* That was stupid and wrong. Don't judge, Jimmy!

I think all of us are tempted to place too much emphasis on how we look on the outside instead of examining where we are in our life on the inside, where we need character and integrity. I don't want to judge the millions of people worldwide who have used Botox or plastic surgery to improve their looks.

Not everyone is on board, though. A number of actors and actresses have expressed disdain with artificially enhancing one's looks. One of them is the elegant Meryl Streep, who said she would never have the wrinkles in her forehead removed because they are the result of her amazement at the beauty of life, or those on her mouth, because they show how much she laughed and how much she kissed. Not even the black spots under her eyes, because behind them she holds precious memories of sadness and crying.

"They are part of me and I love their beauty," Streep has said. "I will preserve my facial features because they're an indication of my life experiences."

LeBron James is one of the greatest basketball players of all time. He often receives negative publicity for taking a stand, which others may not like to accept. I am tempted on some of the issues to judge LeBron, although I'm reminded of the many good things he does, especially for numerous kids and families in his hometown of Akron, Ohio.

In 2004 he started the LeBron James Family Foundation, where he commits his time, resources, and efforts to help many people. He has donated millions of dollars to helping at-risk children and providing encouraging messages to the students at the school he founded there.

LeBron, like me, has made mistakes in his life. That's when I remind myself that I am flawed and very imperfect. I have made my share of poor decisions; hopefully I can learn from them. LeBron is often compared to Michael Jordan, and as a result, there are many hecklers who will boo him in NBA arenas.

It's easy for me to show appreciation and to be grateful to LeBron for the favors he has extended to me throughout the years. Twice we auctioned off dinners with LeBron for our Celebrity Fight Night Charities that sold for over $100,000 each. One of the dinners was hosted at the Wynn Las Vegas hotel. The other was held in LeBron's hometown of Akron.

The second dinner was purchased by a father for his son, a kid who went to a private high school in Arizona known as Brophy Prep. The dinner was scheduled for 6:30 p.m., and we got there in plenty of time. Everything was running like clockwork.

Then my phone rang. It was my cue that LeBron was arriving. I went outside to meet him and escort him inside the restaurant. LeBron looked at me, and I could immediately tell something was wrong.

"Jimmy, I can't do this," he said. "I don't feel good."

Oh no, I thought. "LeBron, you have to do this," I implored. "This gentleman we have seated inside was so generous, and his son is so excited. He took him out of school in Phoenix just to come here. You've got to try to make this happen, even if you can only stay for thirty minutes since I know you don't feel well."

Finally, LeBron relented. He agreed to sit with us through dinner, and he stayed for almost two hours. He was all class, very attentive. I was extremely appreciative of his efforts.

Two days later, I read in the newspaper that LeBron had tested positive for Influenza A, better known as the swine flu. I had to call the donor. I told him, "You know, you might want to see your doctor . . ."

LeBron has helped tremendously with our charities, and I have never been tempted to find any fault with him, even though he occasionally receives criticism.

Temptations are one of the biggest challenges we face on our journey. They are some of the greatest uphill battles we will encounter because we are going to be tested along the way repeatedly, and the Enemy, who is our most persistent tempter, is relentless. We have to resist his temptations constantly, and he doesn't have to bat a thousand to get us off our path.

I'm not saying all of that to discourage you. I am just trying to prepare you for what is coming as you begin walking through life as a Christian. By being aware of the temptations and how to face them, as well as where your strength comes from, you can walk and grow in faith.

"No temptation has overtaken you except what is common to mankind. And God is faithful; he will not let you be tempted beyond what you can bear. But when you are tempted, he will also provide a way out so that you can endure it." — 1 Corinthians 10:13

Why We Face Temptation

Temptation comes in many varieties and from places you wouldn't expect.

It's tempting to take the easy way out, to tell a lie, to hold back the truth, to feel sorry for yourself, or to become discouraged.

We are always tempted to worry or be anxious, to become angry and to not watch our tongues.

I'm constantly tempted to let my mind wander and get pulled off task with distractions that keep me from taking time to pray or hear God when He speaks to me. And sometimes I am tempted to be disobedient because I like to be the one in charge—to be calling the shots and to have things my way.

Lust is another powerful, dangerous temptation—it's at the top of Satan's list for ways to destroy believers, and no one is immune. Whether it is sexual lust or the lust for power, money, fame, or anything else, it leads us all to make choices that are destructive to ourselves and our loved ones. This highlights another temptation, which is selfishness. There is nothing more selfish than giving in to behaviors that can hurt others.

I am also often tempted to procrastinate. Many times I say I am too busy to give God time. God wants to do amazing things in and through our lives. Yet most people miss out on God's blessing because they don't make time for Him in their schedule. They are simply too busy with their own agenda.

Among all of these temptations, jealousy is one of the most universal and destructive we face. Let's be honest: we all are tempted to become jealous. Jealousy caused Lucifer to rebel against God. It's what stirred Cain to kill Abel, and it's what prompted Jacob's sons to sell their brother Joseph into slavery. It's also why King Saul devoted his life to killing David. And why the Jewish leaders handed Jesus over to Pilate to be crucified.

It is not hard to see how giving in to temptation causes a lot of difficulties and can really hurt us. Temptation will be one of the greatest obstacles along the way as you walk in faith, but it is not something that has to block your path.

With all of the trouble that comes from temptation, why do we have to face this challenge over and over, even when we are Christians and have invited Jesus into our hearts? Why is it such an uphill battle?

Too often, we are tempted because we get into vulnerable positions and set ourselves up for a fall. We hang out with the wrong people at the wrong time, thinking of doing the wrong thing. And then we wonder why things are going wrong in our lives.

Christians are usually sincere, well-intentioned people . . . until they are confronted with issues of ego, control, power, money, pleasure, and security. Then we tend to be pretty much like everybody else. This is what makes all of us so susceptible.

"Nothing is more powerful to overcome temptation than the fear of God." — John Calvin

---

We have an enemy who wants to destroy our lives. Even while we are sleeping, Satan is thinking about how to defeat us with temptations and trials, with detours and dead-end streets. He fights with an arsenal of hurts, habits, and hang-ups. And if we try to fight him on our own, that arsenal can leave us beaten up and defeated.

Overestimating our own strength is a common cause of failure. We mistakenly believe we can handle any temptation.

We forget how cunning Satan can be. Remember, he is a master at manipulation. Temptation and condemnation are his favorite methods of breaking us down. First, he tempts us by minimizing sin before it occurs. He'll whisper phrases like "It's no big deal" and "Everyone's doing it." Or he'll say, "Hey, you deserve to have a little fun. Play now and pay up later. Don't worry about the repercussions. You'll be okay. You can trust me." He wages this war on the battlefield of our minds because that is where he can plant these thoughts that allow temptation to grow.

Satan knows that humans are vulnerable, weak, and sinful by nature. And after tempting someone into sin, Satan turns on the condemnation. He tells us, "Well, God will never love you again. Don't even try to reverse course now. It won't matter."

The Bible says a lot about demons and how they want to keep us away from the Word of God. There are demon influences in drugs, alcohol, and sex. They represent a powerful enemy constantly trying to fill our minds with harmful thoughts—fear, worry, discouragement. It's all too easy for Satan to manipulate his way into a seat at the table of your life, a table that is reserved for only you and Jesus.

"Set your minds on things above, not on earthly things." — Colossians 3:2

When God gives you an idea, that's inspiration. But when the devil gives you an idea, that's temptation. Every day, you have to choose which ideas you're going to accept. We need to replace tempting thoughts with biblical truths.

We live hurried lives, and when we are in a hurry, we are tempted to cut corners. This is how we get into so many of our biggest problems that are the easiest to avoid. We cheat to get ahead; we lie to avoid conflict or pain. I didn't want to study the way I needed to for my college class, but I also didn't want to fail and possibly risk getting kicked off the basketball team. That led me to take a shortcut that compromised my integrity and hurt my relationship with God.

When we are in a hurry to get results or to do the things we don't enjoy but are necessary, God gets shuffled to the sidelines. But He wants more than your leftover time and spare moments. He wants to be the center of your life, and that requires taking the time to listen to Him. When we feel pressure to rush things, we get emotional and are moved impulsively, and that creates a barrier to hearing from God. We don't let God's Word sink into the bedrock of our personality, so there's no real change. I want to assure you that being tempted is a very human condition, and that's okay. Being tempted isn't the sin; yielding to the temptation is where we fall into sin.

Here's the secret to overcoming temptation: Don't fight it—refocus.

If we aren't listening to God and open to change, giving in to temptations can get more of a stronghold on our lives and can even become addictions that tear our lives apart.

The Bible doesn't tell you to resist temptation. It tells you to resist the devil (James 4:7), and that's a whole different issue. The key to overcoming temptation is not to push back. It's to change your focus altogether. Why? Because whatever you resist, persists. Whatever gets your attention, gets you.

The battle for sin always starts in the mind. Temptation follows a predictable pattern: attention, activation, and action. Your mind gets fixated, your feelings kick in, and then you act on it. However, if you're focused on God's truth, you are not allowing your mind to drift into areas it has no business going.

The key is to change your mind. Don't try to fight a temptation; instead, turn your mind to God's truth.

The problem is that capturing every thought and turning it to Christ isn't easy. It takes practice. You can't always control your circumstances, and you can't always control the way you feel, but you can choose what you think about. And that will change the way you respond to temptation and help you overcome it by God's grace and in His strength.

CHAPTER 4

WHY I FIND IT EASY TO WORRY

"Why worry when you can pray?"

For over a quarter century, I've been planning big events. I've staged luncheons, banquets, parties, after-parties, and parties after the after-parties. Many of them have included celebrities, famous athletes, and America's top business leaders. Let me tell you: It's a different ballgame when you're playing in the arena of the rich and famous, where every detail is crucial, combustible, and potentially lethal. It's easy to get lost in a sea of worry.

For example, in 2009 I wanted to honor Muhammad Ali for all the money he had helped raise for Phoenix charities. But I wanted to honor him in a different way—a way that spoke to his soul. I arranged for a pregame ceremony in early August at Yankee

Stadium before a series against their hated rivals, the Boston Red Sox. I worried the idea might fall short of my expectations.

"Don't take tomorrow to bed with you." — Norman Vincent Peale

---

I knew that Ali had once fought across the street, beating Ken Norton at the old Yankee Stadium, in a fifteen-round unanimous decision in 1976. I knew he would love the energy that comes from being the center of attention in New York, especially when the Red Sox come to town.

The Yankees agreed to the idea, and when the moment arrived, we piled into a golf cart with two rows. Ali sat in front with the driver. I sat in back with Marilyn, the sister of Ali's wife, Lonnie. As we made our way in from the bullpen area, the Yankees showed Ali's boxing highlights on the videoboards above center field. As we journeyed along the warning track, Ali pointed at and waved to the crowd, like he always does. That's when Yankees catcher Jorge Posada stopped us to personally say hello and to shake Ali's hand. The energy in the stadium started to crest.

The cheers grew louder as we approached home plate. Red Sox outfielder David "Big Papi" Ortiz ran all the way in from the outfield to get a better look. Most Yankees players were standing on the top step of their dugout.

At home plate, Ali helped present a pair of awards to the Yankees organization. And that's when Derek Jeter gave Ali a Yankees cap, drawing a broad grin from the Champ, and prompting all the New York players in the dugout to spill onto the field, joining us at home plate. I felt the moment surge out of control.

I worried that the scene was going to be overwhelming. Only Derek Jeter and superstar reliever Mariano Rivera were supposed to be at home plate with Ali. The celebration turned into something far more than what was budgeted, and I worried that the Yankees organization might be mad at me for upstaging a game between two epic franchises. For allowing things to get out of control. It's very difficult for the main event when Ali is on the undercard, and I feared the Yankees would regret the moment they agreed to my idea in the first place.

But the love of Ali and the joy that emanated from that organic moment at home plate was an instant hit in New York City and beyond. That was the power of Ali. And it was proof that sometimes I worry too much.

Too Busy to Be Bothered

On another occasion, I was worried when I picked up Puff Daddy at his hotel in Scottsdale, Arizona, when he wanted to meet Muhammad Ali. When I met up with the artist, also known as Sean Combs (and Diddy), he had an entourage of about four Cadillac Escalades with his security accompanying him to Ali's home. As we pulled into Ali's neighborhood, Combs' security detail was so paranoid. They actually checked out the front and back yards of Muhammad's neighbors. I was worried about what the neighbors would think. My worrying stopped when Combs and Muhammad, along with Ali's wife, Lonnie, and me had an enjoyable visit in Ali's home.

We are always tempted to judge, and we really shouldn't for two reasons: number one, we are not worthy; and number two, we never have enough information. Some people might be tempted to judge Phil Mickelson that he was greedy when he took approximately $200 million to partner with LIV Golf. Today, Phil is in the neighborhood of being a billionaire. Frankly, to be honest, I am more of a traditionalist. I would have preferred for Phil to continue playing only with the PGA. However, Phil has been a good friend over the years, and I prefer not to be tempted to judge him. I want to be loyal to my friends. I may not always agree with their decisions, just as they might not agree with mine, plus I am aware that the media can really butcher celebrities and tear them apart.

Phil once contributed $500,000 to the Celebrity Fight Night charity event. He allowed us to auction off a round of golf with him in Rancho Santa Fe, California. These important proceeds helped us to develop the Muhammad Ali Parkinson Center in Phoenix. I also remember a time I heard from the Make-A-Wish Foundation that an eight-year-old boy with bone cancer wished he could hit golf balls with Michelson on a driving range. I immediately called Phil, and without hesitation he said yes, he would be happy to meet this boy and hit some golf balls with him. Phil not only hit golf balls with him on the driving range; he played eighteen holes with the boy *and* treated him to lunch.

Once I introduced former heavyweight champion Ken Norton to actor Chevy Chase when Chevy was being honored by Muhammad Ali at Celebrity Fight Night. When Chevy spilled his glass of red wine all over Ken's sport jacket, I worried that Ken might get mad. I was confident he wasn't going to pick a fight with the comedian, but I was very uptight. Ken was gracious, of course.

I also remember being worried and nervous when Nancy and I were invited to join Phil Michelson and his wife, Amy, along with Tom Lehman his wife, Melissa, for dancing lessons. Believe me, dancing was *way* out of my comfort zone, although I thought if Phil and Tom agreed, then I would give it a shot. The lessons were actually really fun and a reminder that we get nowhere by worrying; it only fills us with stress, which is never productive.

Over twenty-five-plus years working under a microscope, I have learned that worrying is a waste of time—it's the act of stewing without doing. We should be too busy to worry during the daytime and too tired to worry at night. Worrying is the opposite of faith because it means we are forgetting that God is in control. Persistent worry should be a spiritual red flag telling you that God is not close enough in your daily journey.

"The reason why worrying kills more people than work is that more people worry than work." — Robert Frost

---

The Roots of Worry

And why do we worry? It's simple. We live in a stressful world. Daily life is so competitive and complex that it's hard not to fret about your job status, your finances, and the people you love. How can you not worry when you have cash flow problems and your creditors are calling, or your financial portfolio is collapsing? How can you not worry when a loved one is diagnosed with cancer? When your job is terminated? Or when your safety is at risk? Doubt, panic, and anxiety, which all come from worry, are among Satan's most effective tools, so he is going to create scenarios all around you to cause worries.

The word *worry* comes the Old English *wyrgan*, which means "to strangle." And that's exactly what worry does. It creates mental and emotional strangulation in your life. Worry makes things worse, because when you worry about the future, you cripple yourself in the present, which is exactly what Satan wants.

We need to remember that among the twenty things we worry about in a given day, nineteen of them will never happen. Worrying is a tremendous waste of energy. And when we waste energy, we never reach peak performance or our full potential.

Worrying is trying to play God. It's assuming responsibility for something that God has said He will take care of. Paul reminded us in Philippians 4:19, "And my God will meet all your needs according to the riches of his glory in Christ Jesus."

God knows what's going on in our lives. He knows all of our needs even before we ask. He wants to help us out. We don't need to worry. Here's why:

- **Worry is unreasonable.** Worry exaggerates the problem. Have you noticed that, if somebody says something bad about you, the more you think about it, the bigger it gets? And worry makes it much harder to see the solutions that are available to you.

- **Worry is unnatural.** No one is a born worrier. Worry is learned. Since worry is unnatural, it's also unhealthy. Your body wasn't designed to handle worry. When people say, "I'm worried sick," they're telling the truth. Doctors say that a lot of people could leave the hospital today if they knew how to get rid of guilt, resentment, and worry. Proverbs 14:30 says, "A peaceful heart leads to a healthy body" (NLT).

- **Worry is unhelpful:** Worry cannot change the past, and worry cannot control the future. All it does is mess up today. It makes you miserable. Second, worry doesn't work. Worrying about something you *cannot* change is useless. And to worry about something you *can* change is a waste of time; just go change it!

- **Worry is unnecessary:** God made you, He created you, He saved you, and He put His Spirit in you. Don't you think He's going to take care of your needs? There's no need to worry.

Deciding to eliminate worry isn't as easy as just saying you won't worry anymore. It takes practice and intention, but it is an important step for walking in faith when the road gets rough. It is the first step to preventing your worry from escalating into fear, which has even more power over our mind and gives more power to Satan.

Fear

It's obvious that we can't change the past. But we can definitely ruin the present by worrying about the future. And if we don't stop worry the moment it starts, it can grow into fear. Once we are in fear about things, our ability to act rationally and reasonably tends to go out the window.

We don't ask for input from trusted advisors, and we don't pray. If you're like me, you probably avoid doing these things because you can guess that the answer you'll get is to stop worrying, to not be afraid. And you will most likely be tempted to respond, "That's easy for you to say. You don't know my circumstances!"

Some people believe once you become a Christian you never have any doubts, stress, or worries. That's not true. Peter had faith and yet he panicked in the storm (Matthew 14:29–32). His faith was gone because he had become weak. Fear had overtaken his soul. He let the appearance of the circumstances he was in blind him to the protection he had and he lost faith in the power of Jesus, who was right there with him.

"Worry is essentially a control issue. It's trying to control the uncontrollable. ... But worry never solves anything!" — Rick Warren

---

The reality is, the storm was big and scary, but God's power is much greater, and Peter forgot that because his fear consumed him. Worry takes our mind to some irrational places because we aren't looking at things through the lens of God's love and strength. If we let worry grow and fester, it can become fear that no longer feels like a possibility in the future but a reality in the present that we have to fight. That is what drives us to stop trusting God and take matters into our own hands. When fear overtakes us, our natural reaction is to act hastily and attempt to solve our own problems. When this happens, we can make even bigger messes because we don't slow down enough to think through our actions and their consequences.

Fear can be hard to combat, especially once it has a stronghold on your life. But fear is the playground where the devil has the most fun, where he is the most effective in distorting our thoughts and our perspective. Getting fear reined in is vital for managing the rough spots in your walk of faith.

When you are afraid, the problem isn't your fear. It's what you do with the fear that really matters. Fear is actually an opportunity to grow closer to God, because your fears reveal where you ought to be trusting Him.

The good news is that God has a plan for you to handle your fear. When fear becomes overwhelming, remember to practice the presence of God. God is always with you; it's your job to acknowledge Him.

And remember that worrying is always worse than reality. The fear of failure is worse than failure itself. The fear of rejection is worse than rejection. Today, make a list of your worries. Then give them to God, one by one.

The number-one source of stress in your life is not work—it's worry. Work doesn't keep you up at night; worry does.

God makes clear in the Bible what He thinks about worry. When you worry about something, you are telling God that you don't think He can handle it. Worry is an offense to God. Why do you need to let go of your worry? You know all those things you're stressing, anxious, and worried about? Let them go.

"Do not be anxious about anything, but in every situation, by prayer and petition, with thanksgiving, present your requests to God." — Philippians 4:6

You can lose your job, your health, your reputation, your spouse, and even your mind. But you cannot lose your relationship with Christ. When you put your security in that promise, you can trust God to meet all your needs. If God loved you enough to send Jesus Christ to die on the cross, don't you think He loves you enough to take care of every other need in your life?

God is going to provide. He's going to take care of you. That's a promise. Instead of stressing out, look for Him to meet all your needs.

You can survive forty days without food, three days without water, and eight minutes without air. But you can't last a single second without hope. It's an essential part of life. When hope is gone, life is over.

So where do you turn to find real hope? God is your true source of hope. He is the way to joy, peace, and power in the Holy Spirit. When you take a step of faith, regardless of your fears, you'll find God actively working in your circumstances. Worry will diminish when you step out boldly for God.

The bottom line: Worrying is a total waste of time. It doesn't change anything. All it does is steal your joy and keep you very busy doing nothing—and you are made for so much more than that.

"Whenever we find ourselves worrying, our first action ought to be to get alone with God and worship Him. We must realize that He is big enough to solve our problems." — Warren Wiersbe

---

SCRIPTURE FOR WORRY

"God has said, 'Never will I leave you; never will I forsake you.'" (Hebrews 13:5)

———

"For the Spirit God gave us does not make us timid, but gives us power, love and self-discipline." (2 Timothy 1:7)

———

"Jesus replied, 'What is impossible with man is possible with God.'" (Luke 18:27)

———

"I can do all things through [Christ] who gives me strength." (Philippians 4:13)

———

"Now all glory to God, who is able, through his mighty power at work within us, to accomplish infinitely more than we might ask or think." (Ephesians 3:20 NLT)

———

"My grace is sufficient for you, for my power is made perfect in weakness." (2 Corinthians 12:9)

CHAPTER 5

WHY I KNOW HOW
TO MAKE MISTAKES

"Please don't agree to this: 'I have learned
so much from my mistakes ... I'm
thinking of making a few more.'"

The fantastic singer Michael Bublé has performed twice at Celebrity Fight Night, and he wowed the audience both times. On a separate occasion, I was invited to a luncheon by David Foster on November 16, 2018, when Michael received a star on the Hollywood Walk of Fame. This was a very proud moment for Michael and his wife, Luisana, along with Michael's mom and dad. I appreciated being invited to join them for the special award.

Here's where I made a mistake, and believe me I know how to make mistakes. I asked Michael during the luncheon if he would allow us to auction off a dinner with him at Celebrity Fight Night the following year. Michael, the gentleman that he is—and I have a good relationship with him—said, "Yes, of course Jimmy, no problem."

Looking back, I feel I was wrong to ask Michael for a favor at his special luncheon. After all, I was lucky enough to be on the invite list without wanting something for myself and our charity event. Things worked out in the end, but I regretted it, and throughout life I have tried to learn from the mistakes I've made like that one.

I am not sure whether this is a mistake or not, although I was quite embarrassed: Nancy and I were in the lobby of Disneyland Hotel in Anaheim when I spotted baseball great Joe DiMaggio. I introduced myself to the former Yankees superstar and told him how much I respected him. As Joe was thanking me for my kind words, I saw my wife and daughter approaching.

"Nancy, I'd like you to meet Joe DiMaggio," I said.

Then I turned to my daughter.

"Jennifer, this is the greatest baseball player of all time, Joe DiMaggio!" I said.

My daughter was five years old. With pigtails and dimples, she looked up at DiMaggio.

"No he isn't, Daddy!" she said. "You told me Reggie Jackson was the greatest!"

Oops.

Another time I made a mistake, frankly it was because I was selfish, because I wanted to sit next to Blake Shelton at our Celebrity Fight Night. Blake is a well-known country music star who is also a huge fan of the Arizona Cardinals. I later learned that Bruce Arians, former head coach of the Cardinals, was really upset and disappointed with me.

Arians was a marquee attraction in the NFL and immensely popular in Arizona. He expected to sit next to Blake, given their mutual interests and star power. I had forgotten they were good friends.

Anyone who has ever planned a wedding or bar mitzvah understands the peril of creating the seating chart and how many egos are needlessly bruised when they're not sitting at a preferred table. It's a thankless job. But in retrospect, I should have had Coach Arians and Blake Shelton sitting next to each other. This was a turnover on my part.

I also made a mistake with singer Rod Stewart, and he was unhappy with me. It had taken a Herculean effort to land Stewart. But when he showed up at Celebrity Fight Night, he hit me with an unexpected request. He asked to go onstage ahead of schedule. He wanted to perform at 9:00 p.m., earlier than most headliners at events like ours.

I agreed. After all, it was my job to keep superstars happy at Celebrity Fight Night.

In the process, I made the mistake of not seeing the big picture while trying to accommodate a music icon. I should have known that based on the event schedule, I would never be able to fulfill his request. Rod didn't get on stage until 10:15 p.m. He was very upset and even thought about leaving our charity event before performing.

I was embarrassed about my mistake and later apologized to his agent.

Problems and Challenges

Life has a way of throwing curveballs at us. Sometimes we even get hit by the pitch. I know I've been plunked a few times. I have also learned that life is a series of problems. You're either in one currently, just coming out of one, or about to go into another one. That isn't meant to sound fatalistic; it's just the reality of how we experience the world and how it experiences us.

As we walk in this world, we are bound to encounter obstacles. Some of them are self-imposed through the choices we make, and some come from outside of us and aren't of our choosing. Sometimes we can avoid them if we are paying attention and considering our steps carefully; but sometimes they are big roadblocks put on our path to test us and teach us.

We all have bumps along the way because even on the parts of the road that are paved smooth for us, we take missteps that cause us to stumble. That's okay. Everyone faces difficulties, and we don't always navigate them well. The point is to learn from what comes up and do better next time.

Let's talk about some of the ways we can end up stumbling along the way—through problems and challenges or mistakes and missteps—and then look at what God says about that and what we can do to course correct when that happens.

If you're like me, big problems can initially lead to a bout with self-pity. We all feel sorry for ourselves. It's a natural reaction and completely understandable. It's also completely useless. Self-pity and feeling sorry for yourself will solve zero problems. I want to tell you about a time when a pretty big problem came up and what I learned through it.

Early in my career, I got into the nasty business of sports ownership. I became one of the new owners of the Phoenix Racquets—a franchise of the World Team Tennis (WTT), a league founded by the great Billie Jean King. I created a big splash when I recruited and signed Chris Evert. She was the number-one player in the world and one of the greatest tennis champions in history. To promote our team, I hired the polarizing Bobby Riggs, a former Wimbledon champion best known for promoting and losing to King in the 1973 Battle of the Sexes. Later, I staged a 1976 match between the Racquets and a team from the Soviet Union in Plains, Georgia, the hometown of then-president Jimmy Carter.

Problems come in different shapes and sizes. There are potential problems, like the kind I encountered on our way to Plains. Everything was going great. Until it wasn't.

Among other challenges, we were caught in a time crunch and our players had to board a tiny airplane in Atlanta for the 150-mile commute to Plains. We were forced to land on a worn-out dirt runway. Our team was very nervous.

Evert was only twenty-one years old and had already won three major tournaments when I signed her: Wimbledon, the US Open, and the French Open. I had promised her father, Jimmy, that I would keep his daughter safe at all times. I wondered what he might think if he saw her sitting on a small plane approaching a dirty airstrip in rural Georgia.

Fortunately for everyone, the landing was as smooth as could be expected, and the event went well. President Carter's famous beer-drinking brother, Billy, attended. It was a huge success, even drawing public words of praise from the president.

Life can seem terribly unfair at times. That's why I like to reach out to people who are experiencing problems. It's easy to find friends and emotional support during good times. But who is there to encourage you when things aren't going well? When you have nothing to offer?

Everyone gets discouraged. Everyone gets depressed. Even the greatest athletes and celebrities go into slumps. That's when I like to step in and provide words of encouragement.

I was also in over my head when I owned the Phoenix Racquets. I had too much ambition and not enough money. We often think that the world is impressed with our success and how we enjoy our prosperity. But they're actually more impressed by how we, as Christians, handle adversity. I didn't do so well in that regard at first.

I was part of an ownership group that included Dr. Jerry Buss (who later purchased the Los Angeles Lakers and became one of the greatest owners in NBA history, winning ten championships) and Robert Kraft (who later purchased the New England Patriots and built a rare NFL dynasty). Kraft also owned Boston Lobsters and flew in fresh lobster to all of our meetings. Buss might show up at a meeting with a girl on each arm after partying much of the night in Las Vegas. Both men effectively served their internships in World Team Tennis.

"Falling down is part of life. Getting back up is living." — Zig Ziglar

------

Me? I lost my shirt. By early 1978, I was tapped out. There was too much politics in tennis, perpetual scheduling issues with players, issues with agents, and many other problems and challenges. My attorney advised me to file for bankruptcy, but I couldn't do that. I wouldn't do that.

I hope you've never experienced this, but if you have, you know it's really hard when you go broke. It destroys your ego and your confidence. It makes you feel insecure and like a failure. The instinct is to run and hide. I was tempted, but I chose to meet my problem head-on. I decided to stand strong, but it wasn't easy. I ended up making arrangements that allowed me to dig myself out of the hole. Some of my creditors received $1,000 per month, others $100 a month. Some received checks from me for fifteen years. I made a huge financial mistake being undercapitalized. All of them received something every month until everyone was repaid in full. It was painful. But it was important to me.

"You can't go back and change the beginning. But you can start where you are and change the ending." — C. S. Lewis

---

The point is that everyone has problems. It's our perspective and the way we handle them that matters. Some people describe life as a series of hills and valleys. I believe that it's more like two rails on a railroad track. You are the train, and you're clinging to both simultaneously. And at all times you have something good and something bad in your life.

Mistakes and Missteps

Sometimes I think "Mistakes" could be my middle name. There have been times when I have been too impulsive in my decision-making, times when I didn't seek guidance and relied on my own ideas, and times when I didn't disclose the whole truth in hopes of impressing others.

As founder of Celebrity Fight Night in Phoenix, I once invited country music icon Garth Brooks and his wife, Trisha Yearwood, to attend our annual event, but he had no expectations of performing. During the evening, one of the event coordinators came to me, asking if we could get him to perform. Like a fool, I signed off on the idea without asking Garth if he was willing, even if it was only for him to sing one of his songs.

The emcee announced to the gathering that Garth Brooks was in attendance and asked if they would like to hear him sing, without giving him a heads-up. The crowd of twelve hundred people went crazy. Being a true gentleman, Brooks came to the stage and sang his famous hit "Friends in Low Places."

The audience loved it, but I quickly found out that he was not happy with my actions. I had acted without his permission and with no advance notice. I was wrong. After the event, I wrote him an apology letter and sent two checks for his foundation. His grace surprised me. He sent back both checks along with a handwritten note expressing how much he appreciated our charity event.

Often when I make mistakes it is because I did not seek wise counsel from trusted friends or guidance from God. I acted with impatience. Many times, when I made a mistake and shared my error with my wife, Nancy, she would say, "Jimmy, did you pray about this?" I have had to answer no more than once.

"And forgive us our debts, as we also have forgiven our debtors." — Matthew 6:12

On one occasion, I made a major mistake in my dealings with Olympic gold medalist Michael Phelps. In 2023, I got a phone call from a friend who wanted to reach Phelps. I typically have a strict policy about protecting my friends' privacy, especially celebrities, but I made the mistake of giving him Phelps' email address. The swimming legend discovered that I'd given out his contact information and sent me an email saying, "Jimmy, you should know better." I immediately recognized my mistake and was very embarrassed. I apologized to Michael, recognizing I had failed my friend and lost his respect all because I didn't think through the consequences of my actions.

When I owned the Phoenix Racquets, I thought it would be a good idea to have an all-Christian tennis team. I brought the idea to Dr. John Mitchell, pastor of Bethany Bible Church in Phoenix, and assumed he would champion it, especially since one of my clients was Stan Smith, a strong Christian and 1972 Wimbledon champion. Dr. Mitchell listened thoughtfully to my plan. And to my disbelief, he disapproved.

He asked me, "How will you respond when one of your Christian players disputes a call and perhaps gets angry with a referee's decision? Or throws their racquet during a temper tantrum? What if the media attacks you and your players?"

I left his office feeling very discouraged. But I soon realized that Pastor Mitchell was right. I was a newer Christian, young in my faith and overzealous in my ambition to spread the gospel. My eagerness has gotten me into trouble more than once. Thankfully, I sought advice this time and avoided a potential misstep in running this team, but it could have gone the other way. Being excited and exuberant about an idea is great, but it is important to temper that with an outside perspective to make sure you are making good decisions.

There is a big side of me in my flesh that encourages me to cover up mistakes. I've felt humbled and crushed after sinning or making a series of mistakes. There are times when I've blown it and wanted to find the nearest cave and crawl out of sight. But that is not the answer because you can't run from accountability forever, and you don't learn anything by burying your head in the sand. So, how do we deal with the fact that we inevitably make mistakes? What does God tell us about this part of our human nature?

First, God is already aware of all your weaknesses and mistakes, and He is actively working to help you change. It won't happen overnight. The truth is, even though you were given a brand-new nature at the moment of conversion when you received Christ, you still have old habits and patterns that need to be replaced.

Your failures don't surprise God. He expects them. He knows what we are made of—because He created us. God won't stop loving us when we mess up.

The central message of the Bible is this: God doesn't love you because of who you are or what you've done but because of who He is and what He has done.

God made you. He loves you. It's settled! You can't make God love you more. You can't make Him love you less. He loves you just as much on your bad days as He does on your good days. His love is not performance-based.

God understands your failures and He loves you anyway. That's amazing grace.

The Bible has a word for this. It's called *grace*—and it's absolutely amazing. When you understand His grace, you can relax about your failures and have the confidence to take more risks. You may have come to God multiple times for forgiveness on the same issue.

The Christian life isn't a mistake-free life, but it can be a guilt-free life. God understands your failures and He loves you anyway. That's amazing grace.

Just remember this: Nobody is perfect. We all make mistakes. We say wrong things, we do wrong things, but then we get up, we learn, we grow, we move on, we live, and we thank God for always giving us another chance. The biggest mistake that we can make is to be afraid to make one, and perhaps the next biggest is to be afraid to admit one.

SCRIPTURE FOR MAKING MISTAKES

"The LORD makes firm the steps of the one who delights in him; though he may stumble, he will not fall, for the LORD upholds him with his hand." (Psalm 37:23–24)

———

"Therefore I will boast all the more gladly about my weaknesses, so that Christ's power may rest on me." (2 Corinthians 12:9)

———

"I tell you, there is rejoicing in the presence of the angels of God over one sinner who repents." (Luke 15:10)

CHAPTER 6

WHY I FIND IT DIFFICULT TO FORGIVE

"Forgiveness sounds like a good
idea until you have to forgive."

We have all been hurt by others, and most of us recognize forgiveness is the right choice and can give it ... as long as the other person apologizes first. There is a big problem with that logic. The offender might never apologize. The offender might not realize the damage he or she has caused. If that's the case, we are left with unresolved conflict, and that interferes with our fellowship with God. The Bible even says that our prayers are hindered by unresolved tensions we may have with others. Forgiveness must be unconditional, and forgiveness must come first.

Do you remember Ivan Boesky?

He was involved in a Wall Street insider trading scandal in the mid-1980s. By 1986, he had amassed more than $200 million by betting on corporate takeovers. He was also featured on the cover of *Time* magazine.

But only the next year, in 1987, he was in prison, sentenced to three and a half years at Federal Correctional Institute Lompoc in California. He was also fined $100 million.

I began reading numerous articles about Boesky. Some stories indicated that he was seeking redemption and forgiveness. That caught my eye.

I decided to visit him in prison. I contacted Lompoc to see how I could obtain permission. I wrote to Boesky several times and he wrote me back. In his letters, he expressed regret and disappointment. Eventually he invited me for a prison visit.

When I met Boesky in prison, we talked about his feelings, his sorrow, and his sense of guilt. We prayed together, and he said he felt relief. I told him to focus on his fresh start and the things that he could control. I have always agreed with C. S. Lewis that you can't go back and change the beginning, but you can start where you are and change the ending.

There is no better example on earth of forgiveness than that of how Jesus offered His forgiveness.

He forgave the Jews who called for His death. He forgave the Romans who nailed Him to the cross. He even forgave every chief priest, elder, and crowd member shouting for His death. Jesus forgave them, which means they were not held guilty for His death.

Jesus said in the parable of the unforgiving servant that it is not enough simply to forgive someone seven times, but seventy times seven (Matthew 18:21–22), which implies as often as is needed.

The Bible also teaches us, "Be kind and compassionate to one another, forgiving each other, just as in Christ God forgave you" (Ephesians 4:32); "For if you forgive other people when they sin against you, your heavenly Father will also forgive you" (Matthew 6:14); and "Bear with each other and forgive one another if any of you has a grievance against someone" (Colossians 3:13).

Nelson Mandela also taught the world about forgiveness. He famously forgave his oppressors. After the end of apartheid, which had fostered racial separation and kept Black people impoverished, Mandela became South Africa's first Black president.

After twenty-seven years in prison, Mandela was freed in 1990 and negotiated with State President F. W. de Klerk the end of apartheid in South Africa, bringing peace to a racially divided country and leading the fight for human rights around the world.

Mandela had plenty of reasons to allow hatred and bitterness to control his life after being in prison for almost three decades. Instead, he is a famous example of forgiveness.

I recall a time I was watching the television broadcast of an international tennis tournament and heard one commentator ask his partner, "How would you rate [person's] serve on a scale of 1 to 10?" The other commentator answered, "8.5, and by the way, I don't believe in a perfect 10." In other words, attaining perfection is often elusive.

The apostle Paul said, "Each of us must bear some faults and burdens of his own. For none of us is perfect!" (See Romans 3:23.) He also wrote in Philippians 3:12–13, "I don't mean to say that I have already achieved these things or that I have already reached perfection. But I press on to possess that perfection for which Christ Jesus first possessed me. No, dear brothers and sisters, I have not achieved it, but I focus on this one thing: Forgetting the past and looking forward to what lies ahead" (NLT).

When Paul wrote this scripture, he was an older man in a Roman prison. He was at the end of his life. He was incredibly mature. Yet he also said he hadn't arrived. If anybody had the right to say, "I've arrived spiritually," it would be the guy who wrote so much of the New Testament. But Paul knew he was still growing, learning, and becoming more like Christ. I want you to remember this because walking in faith does not mean being perfect. We are all going to fall short. We've already covered the ways we will stumble along the way and face uphill battles. Those are natural and normal parts of living in the flesh, and I don't want you to be discouraged and distracted from the path based on a false expectation that being a Christian means being perfect. We aren't perfect; we're just forgiven.

And since we're not perfect, we shouldn't pretend to be. People don't need you to be perfect. They need you to be real with all of your feelings, faults, and fears so they know they aren't alone and can maybe learn from you.

God doesn't need you to be perfect either. If we were perfect and never sinned, there would be no need for His grace. Grace is God's forgiveness for the many ways we prove we aren't perfect. And He asks us to give the same to those around us who come up short.

Why We Need to Give and Receive Forgiveness

Forgiveness is a bedrock principle of Christianity. God calls on us to grant mercy to those who seek forgiveness. He instructs us to forgive our enemies—a concept I struggle with on occasion—and to recognize that everybody is flawed, and we will never have to forgive anyone more than God has forgiven us.

When Jesus was being crucified, He forgave the people who nailed Him to the cross. He didn't wait for an apology. We can remember His example when we are struggling to forgive. There are times when we need to extend that unmerited love and that extra heaping of grace, even when the recipient probably deserves far less.

Remember: "EGR" = Extra Grace Required, instead of "EGO" = Edging God Out

I've had many times when I was unwilling to forgive in moments when I've been deeply hurt, and extending grace to someone else was very hard to do. Once, I invited Tiger Woods to sit courtside with me at a Suns game. He graciously accepted, bringing along his best friend and fellow Stanford golfer, Jerry Chang. Later I heard that a few Arizona-based golf professionals were bad-mouthing me for bringing in a hotshot like Tiger at the expense of the local guys. I couldn't believe the pettiness, and I wanted to be petty right back to them. I had to make a very tough decision: Will I follow the Lord? Or will I remain bitter, angry, and resentful? My desires were betraying me, pushing me toward revenge. But I have learned to experience God's love and forgiveness through Jesus. I have found power in the Holy Spirit. I have learned those wounded moments only lead to more pain and distance from God. I was able to bite my tongue and forgive them, but I had to remember why it is just as important to give forgiveness as it is to receive it.

When we don't forgive others, resentment can grow, and that makes us miserable, keeping us trapped in the past. And when we're stuck in the past, we are controlled by the past.

"If we confess our sins, he is faithful and just and will forgive us our sins and purify us from all unrighteousness." — 1 John 1:9

There is no better example of this than former Phoenix Suns head coach Monty Williams, who lost his wife in a tragic car accident when he was coaching in Oklahoma City in 2016. Ingrid Williams, age forty-four, was driving with three of their five children when she was struck by another car. Both drivers perished in the crash.

The other driver had a history of speeding violations and lost control of her SUV, jumping the center line and crashing into Ingrid. An autopsy revealed she had amphetamines in her system.

At Ingrid's funeral, her husband did the most amazing thing—he forgave the woman who killed his wife. He also asked that all of his sympathizers pray for everyone involved. It was an amazing show of grace.

Williams said, "I want to close with this, and I think it's the most important thing we need to understand. Everyone is praying for me and my family, which is right. But let us not forget that there were two people in this situation. And that family needs prayer as well, and we have no ill will towards that family.

"In my house, we have a sign that says, 'As for me and my house, we will serve the Lord.' And we cannot serve the Lord if we don't have a heart of forgiveness. That family didn't wake up wanting to hurt my wife. Life is hard. It is very hard, and that was tough, but we hold no ill will toward the Donaldson family. And we, as a group, brothers united in unity, should be praying for that family because they grieve as well. So, let's not lose sight of what's important."

The entire Oklahoma City Thunder basketball team was at the funeral and saw a beautiful example of forgiveness from their head coach.

Williams recently retold his story on a virtual broadcast that I host with NBA icon Jerry Colangelo. His act of forgiveness is just as amazing now as it was when he lost his wife, and the anguish and pain made him consider retirement from the NBA coaching ranks. Yet, in all that pain, Williams still found strength to walk by faith.

"You never so touch the ocean of God's love as when you forgive and love your enemies." — Corrie ten Boom

---

He could have refused to forgive. I don't think anyone would blame him for that. But he saw the wisdom in not harboring resentment. He knew that resentment is self-torture. It destroys your relationships, robs you of peace and joy, and prevents you from moving forward in your life. I want to say for the record, though, that forgiveness isn't the same as trust. When someone hurts you, forgiveness is required by God; but that doesn't mean you need to trust that person like you did before. Just because you forgive someone, it doesn't mean you are obligated to have them in your life after that.

But if you hang on to resentment and don't forgive, it doesn't just hurt your human relationships; it also infects your relationship with God. If you are still carrying wounds from those who hurt you ten, twenty, or even thirty years ago, you are allowing that hurt to fester to this very day. Don't let that happen. You can learn from a hurtful experience—but you must let it go so they can't hurt you anymore.

In his book *Open Doors*, Pastor Rick Warren wrote about how we need to let go of our pain, our hurt, and our bitterness. Our response to evil should be acts of kindness and goodness. When we need to make peace with someone and refuse to do so, our happiness suffers because we can't be happy and in conflict at the same time.[1]

Peacemaking is a priority, whether we are the offender or the offended. This is a hard step, but the longer we wait to make peace, the more difficult it will become. When we need to make the peace, it is important to do everything in our power to bring restoration.

If we are being honest, we must admit that we've all needed to seek forgiveness from God for a failure or two in the past. In fact, we might have asked so many times we start to wonder how much forgiveness God is willing to give us. How many times is He willing to pardon our imperfections? How many second chances do we get? Thankfully, there is no limit to the grace of God.

I know God's standards are high and I have often fallen short of them, and I have had to ask Him to forgive me. Especially when

- my priorities, actions, and decisions are made to exalt myself, placing me above the Lord;
- I care more about my own reputation than God's reputation;
- my love for Him doesn't come first;
- I fail to spend time in prayer or reading the Bible and instead waste time on things that have no eternal value;
- I have lost control of my emotions, my thoughts, and my words, leaving wounds on the hearts of those around me;
- I am inadequate and use that as an excuse for disobedience;
- I allow others to think I'm more spiritual than I really am.

I ask for so much forgiveness that I would be a hypocrite not to extend the same grace to others.

Forgiveness is a two-way street, which means you cannot receive what you are unwilling to give. Jesus said, "If you forgive those who sin against you, your heavenly Father will forgive you. But if you refuse to forgive others, your Father will not forgive your sins" (Matthew 6:14–15 NLT).

Someone once told theologian John Wesley, "I could never forgive that person!" To which Wesley replied, "Then I hope you never sin."

Just as important, real forgiveness is unconditional. There's no attachment to it. You don't earn it; you don't bargain for it. Forgiveness is not based on a promise to never repeat the offense again. You forgive because it follows Jesus' example. As Pastor Rick Warren stated, "When Jesus stretched out His hands on the cross and said, 'Father, forgive them, for they do not know what they are doing' (Luke 23:34), nobody had earned it or asked for it. Jesus took the initiative and offered forgiveness."

On our own power, this kind of forgiveness isn't possible. But the power to forgive comes from Jesus. Remember God's unconditional love for you, and express that love to those who hurt you. Recognize that no one is perfect. When we have been hurt, we tend to lose our perspective about the person who offended us. But we need to remember that we are all imperfect people.

It's very important to relinquish your right to get even. Choose compassion over any temptation to retaliate. The Lord will enable you to respond to evil with good. Getting even only brings you down to the other person's level. Take the high road instead. The Bible says to treat your enemies with kindness. It's nearly impossible to do this on your own. That's why you need the love of Jesus to fill you up.

As an old saying goes, "You are not grown up until you know how to communicate, apologize, be truthful, and accept accountability without blaming someone else."

And as Rick Warren reminded us, "If God used perfect people, nothing would get done. God will use anybody if we are available."

It's not our ability as much as our availability. We are all flawed. And that, my friends, is where grace comes in!

SCRIPTURE FOR FORGIVENESS

"If we confess our sins, he is faithful and just and will forgive us our sins and purify us from all unrighteousness." (1 John 1:9)

———

"Be kind and compassionate to one another, forgiving each other, just as in Christ God forgave you." (Ephesians 4:32)

———

"Remember, the Lord forgave you, so you must forgive others." (Colossians 3:13 TLB)

———

"If you forgive those who sin against you, your heavenly Father will forgive you. But if you refuse to forgive others, your Father will not forgive your sins." (Matthew 6:14–15 NLT)

CHAPTER 7

WHY I NEED TO SHOW PEOPLE LOVE

"The greatest religion in the world is the religion of love." — MUHAMMAD ALI

*L*ove is the most powerful tool we can bring to any situation. And when we put our time and energy into helping others or serving God, we are showing the greatest love we can offer. Love heals, uplifts, strengthens, energizes, refreshes, and renews.

John Harper, a Scottish Baptist pastor and a widower, was aboard the RMS *Titanic* when it struck an iceberg and sank. He put his young daughter and niece in a lifeboat and stayed behind to preach the gospel to fearful passengers. As the Titanic was about to sink, he finally jumped into the freezing water but did not survive. Being the caretaker of two young children, he could have claimed a seat in a lifeboat, but he gave his life for others.

Harper displayed, according to Jesus, the greatest love one can show: laying down one's life for his friends (John 15:13). Eternity will no doubt reveal those who found eternal life because a faithful pastor gave his life for them. In that way, Harper imitated the sacrifice of Christ, who gave His life that we might live. Yet we can demonstrate the "greatest love" in countless other ways when we die to our own desires and choose the good of another over ourselves.

How can you put that into practice? It doesn't have to be complicated. Look for an opportunity today to demonstrate Christ's "greatest love" for the sake of another. Our job is to love people we don't have to love.

Over two decades, I spent many hours doing charity work with Muhammad Ali. I never saw him refuse an autograph or be unwilling to have his picture taken with a fan. I never heard Ali say a bad word about anyone. Why? Because the Champ practiced what he preached. He practiced love with all people.

I had met Ali in 1985. He was having dinner with Sammy Davis Jr. and Jerry Buss, owner of the Los Angeles Lakers, at the Forum Club before a Lakers game. When we were introduced I said, "Muhammad, we have a mutual friend in Earnie Shavers."

To my surprise, Ali said nothing.

I repeated my words.

Again, nothing.

I tried one last time.

"Champ, Earnie loves you a lot," I said.

"If he loved me so much, why did he hit me so hard?" Ali responded with his trademark twinkle in the eye and wry smile.

Ali is one of the few people in history to go from being hated to being loved. He stood for something bigger than boxing and was known for his openness, sense of humor, and natural charisma. Inside the ring he was perhaps the greatest boxer ever; outside of it, he loved people as much as any friend I have ever had. His love made him a world-renowned peace advocate and humanitarian dedicated to improving people's lives. He was much more than a three-time heavyweight champion boxer. He was a life champion, showing love for the poor, the children, the sick, and the elderly. Ali couldn't spell the word *hate*, since it was not in his vocabulary.

Much of my work is with charities. It's easy to love people who are always there to help you. Several examples of people I've found easy to love would be Muhammad Ali, David Foster, Reba McEntire, and Andrea Bocelli.

I have mentioned Celebrity Fight Night several times already. I started the charity event in 1994 with Charles Barkley. Several years later, I began partnering with Muhammad Ali and did so for twenty years before he passed. Muhammad never once said no to me; every time I asked him for some help for our charity, his answer was always yes. When you realize that the Champ was perhaps the most recognized person in the world for many years, people were always asking him for favors. I realized I was blessed for the love he gave me with our friendship.

David Foster, a sixteen-time Grammy winner, is also an easy guy to love. We did twenty-two consecutive Celebrity Fight Night events in Phoenix, and to date he and I have done five events together in Italy. David, just like Ali, Reba, and Andrea, has never said no to me, and I have never said no to David for whatever he needed. It's truly a love-love relationship.

Reba McEntire is an easy person for Nancy and me to love for many reasons. Reba did sixteen consecutive Celebrity Fight Nights, along with five events in Italy plus some other local charity events. This lady is at the top of the list when it comes to superstar entertainers who are humble. Why? Because she gives back.

Andrea Bocelli is a special friend living in Italy. He and his wife, Veronica, are easy to love with the ways they always help me and many others throughout the world. We continue to do charity events together in Italy and Phoenix. Both Andrea and Veronica are a package of love for everyone. They embody the truth of Scripture that says three things remain—faith, hope, and love—and the greatest of these gifts is love (1 Corinthians 13:13).

Mother Teresa was often criticized because of her strong faith in God and devoted Christian beliefs; however, she didn't let that deter her, pointing out that if we judge people, we don't have time to love them.

We know in this world some people are very difficult to love. Mother Teresa knew that Jesus has given us grace, which is unconditional love, and she knew that in serving the Lord she needed to offer that same grace and unconditional love to others.

Mother Teresa treated everyone with compassion and supported them regardless of their religious beliefs or social status. Why? Because she lived her life as a picture of love. She was loving because it was the suffering of the poor that taught her what she was to do and how she was to do it; it was her love for Christ, who loved them first, that made her faithful to them.

Throughout her inspiring life, Mother Teresa stressed the need to care for the poor, the suffering, and the unwanted as a route to peace. "The poor must know that we love them, that they are wanted."

It is important to ask God, "How can I bless someone else today?" That is an incredible act of love that will fill their life and yours.

If you just aren't ready to turn your attention to someone else because you are fighting discouragement, doubt, or despair, at least try to shift your eyes off of your problems and onto all the good things God has done in your life. You can even write them down and make a list! You'll be amazed at all you come up with, and it will serve as a reminder to you in the days ahead.

You will have seasons of doubting God's love for you. This is a natural part of your spiritual maturity. When this happens, remember that God loves you even when you don't feel it. But you can't just know about God's love; you need to personally experience it. And the best way to do this is to let Him have control, let Him guide you and teach you, let Him be the source of your peace.

God wants us to love Him with all of our heart, soul, mind, and strength (Matthew 22:37). In fact, Jesus called that the most important commandment. You have the ability to love God with all yourself because you were made in the image of God, and the greatest part of Him is love.

The Lord is working in our circumstances to align all the details to His will—to develop our patience, perseverance, character, and optimism. God works as we're waiting, so trust Him even in times of little observable progress. In due time, He will give the victory! God has promised to give you peace of mind. Accepting His peace doesn't mean your life will be problem-free. It means that even when your world seems to be falling apart, you will be able to think clearly and sleep peacefully. You will know you are standing on solid ground.

Peace is not something you work for or beg for. It's a gift you receive by faith. Turn to God in prayer and tell Him what's on your mind. Focus on His goodness, and His perfect peace will fill your heart and mind. If you're going through a dark valley and you're under a lot of stress, you can choose to trust God. He is faithful even in the shadows, where things may not make sense and where it can seem like a long, long way out of the valley.

There are some people who I might not like, but I do *love* them. The same love God gives to you, He wants you to offer to everyone around you. It's not an option or a suggestion. It's a command from Jesus: "Now I am giving you a new commandment: Love each other. Just as I have loved you, you should love each other" (John 13:34).

"Love never gives up, never loses faith, is always hopeful, and endures through every circumstance." — 1 Corinthians 13:7 NLT

If you are a follower of Christ, you must love everybody—whether you like them or not—in the same way Christ loves you. That means you are to accept them completely, love them unconditionally, forgive them totally, and consider them extremely valuable.

It is such an encouragement to know that God never stops loving you. God will always be patient with you, believing in you, and hoping for the best in your life. God never gives up on you.

And that's what God wants you to do with everybody else: loving them in ways that will transform your life and your relationships.

SCRIPTURES ON THE IMPORTANCE OF LOVE

"And now these three remain: faith, hope and love. But the greatest of these is love." (1 Corinthians 13:13)

———

"Love is very patient and kind, never jealous or envious, never boastful or proud, never haughty or selfish or rude. Love does not demand its own way. It is not irritable or touchy. It does not hold grudges and will hardly even notice when others do it wrong." (1 Corinthians 13:4–7 TLB)

———

"No matter what I say, what I believe, and what I do, I'm bankrupt without love." (1 Corinthians 13:3 MSG)

———

"We remember before our God and Father your work produced by faith, your labor prompted by love." (1 Thessalonians 1:3)

———

"We love because he first loved us." (1 John 4:19)

CHAPTER 8

WHY I NEED TO
SET GOALS

"I am still working on my PhD degree:
pride, humility, and discipline."

*M*y goal when I owned the Phoenix Racquets in World
Team Tennis (WTT) was to turn our franchise into a
good investment. We led WTT in attendance. Yet somehow, I lost
about $2 million in my role as general partner.

We had some big contracts, but I didn't go into the venture
as a classic rich boy. I was just a hard worker from the insurance
business. At one point, Reggie Jackson said I was keeping the franchise together with Band-Aids.

At another point during my ownership, I was seriously undercapitalized. I needed a $50,000 line of credit just to be seated at
a WTT league meeting. I couldn't pull it off. I was embarrassed

and humbled. The guy who signed tennis star Chris Evert to a two-year contract couldn't even be seated at the league meeting.

During one meeting, the owners were getting rough with me. But Jerry Buss, another WTT owner who last purchased the Los Angeles Lakers, had my back. He stood up and said, "Hold on. Jimmy went out and put us on the map by signing the number-one tennis player in the world." They argued a lot—that's what owners do when they get together. And that's when Buss said to the entire room, "I believe in Jimmy. And I'm going to back him."

He walked out of the meeting. Then he and I went for coffee and he told me he would cover me for the $50,000. You don't forget gestures like that. Especially when I had known Jerry Buss for only three weeks!

One of my goals is I want my friends who are Jewish to know that I support and love Israel. Billy Crystal has commented more than once that he is grateful that I helped him fund his theater program Peace Through the Performing Arts at the Hebrew University of Jerusalem. We gifted $500,000 from Celebrity Fight Night to the university.

Billy introduces me as his "Gentile friend." Once I asked him, "Why do you introduce me that way? I don't introduce you as my Jewish friend." Billy replied, "Because you have blond hair and blue eyes!" (By the way, Billy told me his golf game is a lot like Israel—we both have trouble in the sand!)

I have only one award displayed in my office. Sitting on my desk is the American Jewish Committee's National Human Relations Award from 1982. The gift is a three-foot statue of the prophet Isaiah. This award is very meaningful to me because Isaiah was the greatest prophet of them all. Isaiah means a lot to me as a Christian, just like my rabbi friend in Los Angeles who couldn't wait to tell me he had written my name on a piece of paper and placed it in the Wailing Wall in Jerusalem. Years ago I purchased

Israel Bonds. Jerusalem is the city of God, the city He loves more than any other (Psalm 87:1).

It's All about Others

My goal, when it comes to hospitality, is to think more about the other person than myself. However, I pretty much blew it at a Phoenix Suns game when I had football star Jake Plummer as my guest.

The Suns, playing the Boston Celtics, were behind by twelve points with fifty seconds left in the fourth quarter. I tried to talk Jake into leaving so we could beat the crowd. Jake said, "No way, Jimmy, there's still almost a minute left, and the Suns can come back and win."

Jake was an All-American quarterback at Arizona State University and then a star with the Denver Broncos. He understood clock management much better than I did, plus he was well known for coming back to win games when his teams looked like they were going to lose.

Jake said, "Jimmy, there's two people in the sports arena that know the Suns can win the game: Jason Kidd [an All-Star player with the Suns] and me."

I said, "Okay, Jake, I agree." The Suns still lost, although they almost won in the last second. Jake was right, and I was wrong. I was honestly thinking more of myself than what my guest preferred.

One of my goals is to help people who have problems. I became friends with Sam Walton by merely writing him a letter, and we exchanged numerous letters before I was invited to meet with him in Bentonville at the home office of Walmart.

During our breakfast meeting at Days Inn in Bentonville, Sam told me about his four-year-old grandson, Luke, who had a life-threatening cancer. Sam also shared that Luke was a huge Michael Jordan fan. After our meeting I contacted Michael. I told him about Walton's grandson and asked if he wouldn't mind sending an autographed basketball for young Luke. Michael agreed, and I gave that ball to Sam to give to his grandson. I love being a facilitator in situations like that, connecting a pair of megawatt celebrities through a simple gesture.

My goal at Celebrity Fight Night was to help numerous charities in Phoenix. We gave away approximately $100 million over twenty-seven years, and it was important for Nancy and me to make certain our program was always clean, respectful, and in good taste.

Billy Crystal often came to our charity event, and several times he brought his good friend Robin Williams. We decided to honor Robin with the Muhammad Ali Award during the evening. We also knew that Robin was very capable of rattling off the f-word during his entertaining.

In advance, I spoke to our staging manager and asked her to please inform Robin to keep his entertainment fun and clean. By the way, I think Robin was one of the funniest comedians I've ever heard in my life, and certainly among the most beloved by millions. And he did not use the f-word at our charity event.

"A goal is a dream with a deadline." — Napoleon Hill

As we have taken this journey to walk by faith, we have learned how God equips us for dealing with all of the challenges and struggles we will encounter. We know what we need to take with us, but we also have to have a goal and a destination in mind, or we will wander aimlessly.

For Christians, the ultimate destination is heaven, but before we get there, we have a long road to travel and will have a number of stops along the way to do the work God has called us to in this life.

We can't plan everything or anticipate all that will happen, as we've already learned, but we can chart a course that involves setting goals for how we want to live and what we want to accomplish. Those goals are not about how much money we want to earn or how many things we want to acquire. They are about the kind of witness we want to be to others and how we want to serve God. Learning how to set effective goals is important for keeping us on our path and in God's will for our lives, but we often set goals ineffectively or with the wrong ambitions in mind.

Your Checkpoints

I am a man who needs a goal, who wants to make a difference. I have always set ambitious goals. I've been blessed and fortunate enough to attain most of them. And one of my most important goals is to manage my time properly.

I keep calendars. I make appointments. I have daily plans, weekly plans, and plans for the rest of my life. But I have come to understand that not every goal is a godly goal. Now, not every goal you set needs to be, but godly goals are aligned with God's promises in His Word and give you the courage and faith to move forward when it feels much more natural to be scared or uneasy.

"Every goal is only a problem to be solved." — Howard Schultz

---

Most people have a shared experience with goals: they fail. Why? Well, too often, we set the wrong kind of goals. It's not enough to say your goal is to be a better parent. Even if you spend more time with your children, you'll never know if you've completed the goal because it isn't specific.

Studies show that only five percent of Americans have written goals. Those same five percent are also the highest wage earners in the nation. Successful people set their direction and go for it. Unsuccessful people allow life to happen to them. Without goals, they have no idea where they are going, and time just passes them by.

We also know how hard it is to stay enthusiastic day after day, in the face of delays, difficulties, dead ends, problems, pressures, and criticism. It's very difficult to sustain the enthusiasm necessary to make a real impact.

And positive thinking isn't enough. Pulling yourself up by your psychological bootstraps won't cut it. Talking yourself into a state of optimism isn't sustainable. Enthusiasm will ebb and flow with the stock market, the economy, the weather, or your personal circumstances.

We were created to glorify the Lord and to be fruitful in His service. To stay on top of the plan God has for our lives, we should plan times to stop, ask, and listen for guidance. The world throws confusing messages at us all day long, and we need to check our course frequently. These conversations with the Lord are vital for a thriving life of godly impact. Without them, we miss the mark.

Many people shy away from setting goals because the process feels too heavy. Maybe you have avoided setting goals for one of these reasons:

1. You don't know what you want.
2. You don't believe goals work.
3. You confuse activity with accomplishment.
4. You confuse wishes and wants with goals.

5. You're afraid you will fail.

6. You do the urgent and not the important.

7. You don't understand the true function of a goal.

"Your goal always seems impossible until it is done." — Nelson Mandela

---

It's understandable that goal-setting would feel daunting when you aren't clear about their purpose or how they can work best for you.

Now, here are some important questions to ask when you think about setting goals:

1. Where am I?

2. Where do I want to be?

3. How do I know I am getting there?

One of our goals should be trusting that God knows everything about us before it ever happens. God can see past, present, and future all at once. This part of His character is something we can't fully understand, for God is not like us! However, we can take great comfort that He knows everything that has ever happened and will happen.

God knows everything you are going to encounter along your journey, but He's not going to reveal it to you all at once, because you wouldn't be able to handle it. You'd get discouraged by all the difficulties you are going to face, and you'd get prideful over all of the success. God gives you just enough to handle. Just enough to move you to the next checkpoint that draws you closer to Him. God knows what you need.

You trust a doctor with your health because they have great knowledge. Greater still, you can confidently trust God because His knowledge is perfect. Allowing Him to guide you in setting your goals means you won't miss the mark, and the checkpoints you have along the way will keep you aligned with His will and purpose for your life.

Finding Your Course

Colonel Sanders was sixty-two years old when he started Kentucky Fried Chicken. Ray Kroc didn't invent the Big Mac until he was sixty-five. Picasso was still painting at eighty-eight. At eighty-five, Michelangelo was asked when he was going to retire. "When I quit learning," he said.

We should never stop learning. We should never stop dreaming. But you need to set goals because they are the runway for your dreams. Goals allow dreams to take flight. I am always more interested in what I am about to do than what I have already done, so continuing to set goals is a priority for me. But I also make sure the goals I'm setting are godly goals.

"If you want to live a happy life, tie it to a goal, not to people or things." — Albert Einstein

---

When you set a goal that requires faith, you change during the journey to achieve that goal. Having godly goals is what helps us move in the right direction, recover our footing when we stumble, cross over the hills and through the valleys along the way, smooth out the rough spots on the road, and get back on solid ground.

Godly goals give us hope and a reason to endure, even through the most difficult times. They give us contentment, and that makes a huge difference on our perspective and definition of success. When we put God in first place, amazing things happen. When God is your foundation and your priority, that relationship will energize the rest of your life.

It is also important to understand that goals require good planning. These three practices have been the most impactful way for me to achieve my goals:

1. **Steps**: I establish how I am going to get from where I am now to where I want to go. Then I write down these steps.

2. **Deadlines**: I assign a date to each step. A goal is a statement of faith in what I believe God wants me to accomplish. Putting a timeline to my steps forces me to uphold my end of the bargain.

3. **Schedule**: I write those dates on my calendar. I make sure not to hide them in a filing cabinet or under a stack of papers. I put them on my desktop calendar, laptop calendar, and smartphone calendar. I set alerts and updates on every media platform I use in my daily business.

If your goal is to have a healthy body, then maybe you need to keep healthier food in your house or create a meal plan. Maybe you need to commit to regular exercise, even if you start small with fifteen minutes a day.

"If you don't know where you are going, every road will get you nowhere." — Henry Kissinger

---

If your goal is to have a healthy mind, then you may need to unsubscribe from some magazines or block some channels. You may just need to delete some apps or put healthier boundaries around your screen time.

If your goal is to have a clean heart, then you need to spend time in prayer, asking God what you need to confess and then confessing those things. This can be the most difficult step of spiritual cleansing. Through confession, you're recognizing and rooting out sins that cause unhealthy habits throughout your spiritual house.

The point is you not only have to be specific about your goals but you also need to take the right steps to achieve them. Just deciding you want to accomplish something does not make it come to fruition.

I also think goals should be big enough to excite us, yet also realistic, because if they're too big and overwhelming, we'll never reach them. I don't want to live with the goal of just getting by; I want to live with greater significance than personal achievements, accolades, or putting together a terrific bio. How about you? With God's purpose, your life can overflow with meaning. God will reward your priorities. You will find that His wisdom makes the hours of your days more profitable and the rest of your years more fruitful.

"It's kind of fun to do the impossible." — Walt Disney

Ultimately, our goal should be a deeper relationship with God. Not only is that the most important; it's the one that will help us achieve all the others. You can talk to God about your hopes, dreams, fears, anxieties, goals, ambitions, hurts—anything you'd tell a close friend, you can tell God. He wants to hear everything you care about. You can share the things you are embarrassed about, the things you're proud of, and the things you're ashamed of. You can talk to God about every part of your life.

Train yourself to set the right goals, and you will become more efficient and more successful. You might even become unstoppable! Imagine the impact your life could have if you asked God to guide your goals, and then ask Him today, "What do you want me to change about my life? What do you want to accomplish through me? On what and on whom should I focus?"

As another important step, ask God to help you establish goals for the next season. Pray, "God, what do you want to do in my life today? This week? This month? This year? Over the next five years?" Then move forward in faith. God will walk with you and show you how to handle the ups and down of life along the way.

Forging Ahead

Our end goal as Christians is to cross the finish line victorious. A lot of people start out the Christian life with so much promise. They are off and running. But when they collapse and fall, they don't get up. They may crawl off or slow down. Or maybe they round a bend and simply walk away as though they never intended to run the spiritual race.

There will be times in our lives as Christians when we collapse and fall. And when that happens, all we can do is get up again. We may feel like quitting, but if we quit we won't reach our goal to finish the race.

When Paul was approaching the end of his life, he wrote, "As for me, my life has already been poured out as an offering to God. The time of my death is near. I have fought the good fight, I have finished the race, and I have remained faithful" (2 Timothy 4:6–7 NLT).

Notice that he didn't say, "I *ran* the race." No, he said, "I *finished* the race." That is the key. It is not enough to start well; we need to finish well too. It is not enough to run fast; we need to run fast and long. Keep running, because you're going to leave a legacy.

"Aim at heaven and you will get earth thrown in. Aim at earth and you will get neither." — C. S. Lewis

---

Paul wanted to join the ranks of those who had crossed the finish line. He wanted to be in the company of those in God's winner's circle, like Joshua and Caleb in the Old Testament who finished their races well.

Jesus had a goal, and that was to go to the cross. The cross wasn't a mistake. Jesus knew it was coming and spoke of it often. He had to suffer and die because there was no other way to bridge the gap between a holy God and sinful humanity. The cross was Jesus' goal and destination from the beginning.

We are to set aside our own aims, goals, ambitions, and desires in life, giving up our own wills. That is what it is to follow Jesus. This is a long-distance run. So, if you have fallen, it's time to get back up; if you have been slowing down, it's time to speed up again.

My goals as a Christian include consistently praying and reading the Bible. However, it is easy for me to wander away from both of those. Why? Because I let my flesh control my feelings. Many times when I am praying, my mind may drift and I lose my concentration.

My goal is to trust Jesus. I need to practice trusting Jesus more in my life every day. I confess that when my health is good, when my bank account is full, when my friends are many, when my name is well regarded, and when my family is happy, I tend to drift into complacency. Then when trials and tribulations come, I start getting humble and surrender. Often those are God's way of getting my attention. Plus, God promises not to give us more than what we can bear.

Our goal should be to become mature Christians. Some Christians, however, have known the Lord for years yet are still spiritual babies. They need to be spoon-fed spiritual truths. They still need to be dazzled. And they are still looking for something new. It is time to grow up. It's time to be mature people of God, with a faith that sustains us, instead of living on fickle emotions. It is also time to find younger believers and help them grow up to spiritual maturity as well. There are false teachings and other things that can lead us astray. We need to be mature so that we can apply proper biblical understanding.

"In their hearts humans plan their course, but the LORD establishes their steps." — Proverbs 16:9

God is going to give you a goal for your life, and some people may think it's pretty crazy. But you have to stay focused on what you know God has said to you through prayer and through His Word.

God wants to bless your goals. But not every goal you set is a goal that God will bless. How do you know which goals are best?

It's important to determine if your goal will honor God. Goals that bring glory to God are those that cause you to trust Him more. If your goal doesn't require faith, then you don't need God to bless it. You just need to get to work. If you want God's blessings, you need a faith-based goal because the Bible says, "Without faith it is impossible to please God" (Hebrews 11:6).

Determining the motivation of your goal is a big step in the process because God won't bless a goal motivated by greed, envy, guilt, fear, or pride. But He does honor a goal motivated by a desire to demonstrate love to Himself and to others. If you want God's blessing, you also need a love-based goal.

Day by day, the world is unraveling, becoming more frayed and afraid, more unstable and unsteady. We hear of wars and rumors of war, of false Christs, of famines, of earthquakes, and of pestilences. Nations are rising against nations and kingdoms against kingdoms. Christians are attacked and slain at an accelerated pace. But there is a God in heaven.

My goal at this time in my life is summed up in six words: *I want God to use me!* I really don't have any exact plans on how I want the coming year to go. I really just want God to take the lead.

And so my goal starts with staying humble. I admit I am humbled when Billy Crystal says I'm the rare person who just wants to do good, or when Lionel Richie talks about the passion I have for my beliefs, or when Bob Costas says I'm willing to give more for any good cause, or when Kenny Rogers talked about my having a mission to help others, or when Reba McEntire talks about my sincerity, or when Kevin Costner says I'm really a giver, or when Carrie Underwood says I'm a good man, or when Rick Warren says I'm a good Christian.

But that's exactly when I want to stand up and say I am not a perfect Christian with the perfect life. I am a sinner. I am flawed. I am broken. I struggle. And I have fallen more times than I would like to admit.

All of the above is why I need Jesus in my life.

SCRIPTURE FOR CHARTING OUR COURSE

"Do not let any unwholesome talk come out of your mouths, but only what is helpful for building others up according to their needs, that it may benefit those who listen." (Ephesians 4:29)

———

"Reverence for God adds hours to each day." (Proverbs 10:27 TLB)

———

"My thoughts are nothing like your thoughts. . . . And my ways are far beyond anything you could imagine." (Isaiah 55:8 NLT)

———

"Commit to the LORD whatever you do, and he will establish your plans." (Proverbs 16:3)

———

"Trust in the LORD with all your heart and lean not on your own understanding; in all your ways submit to him, and he will make your paths straight." (Proverbs 3:5–6)

CHAPTER 9

WHY I HAVE PROBLEMS

"I have a problem: I'm getting so old that
when I hit a golf ball off the tee I can hear
the ball land." — GOLF CHAMPION GARY PLAYER

*E*very Christian will face problems in life for their own good. Jesus said, "Here on earth you will have many trials and sorrows. But take heart, because I have overcome the world" (John 16:33 NLT). He didn't say you *might* have trials and sorrows; He said you *will* have them. However, God does not allow us to experience trials because He wants to see us suffer. That's not how God operates. As writer Corrie ten Boom once said, "God has no problems, only plans."

"Everything that we have—right thinking and right living, a clean slate and a fresh start—comes from God by way of Jesus Christ." — 1 Corinthians 1:30 MSG

The Bible doesn't say everything is good. Because it's not all good. There is a lot of sin and evil in the world. But God makes it all work for a great purpose for those who love Him and for those who are called to Him. And if you think God can't put back together the pieces of your broken life, you are not giving Him enough credit. God can do anything. And He is still waiting to give you His dream for your life, if you haven't claimed it already.

When I face problems or challenges, I often think of Joseph, who was tested with many trials and temptations. He was thrown into a pit by his brothers and treated poorly. He was given to a slave trader and ended up being punished for things he didn't do. But he did not attempt to get even. He could have easily folded under adversity. Instead, he kept God's grace within him and believed in God's promises with every difficult circumstance. Joseph trusted that God was at work in his life. In the end, Joseph had a rags-to-riches story and ended up in a prosperous and powerful position because He faithfully relied on God's guidance. (Read more beginning in Genesis 37.)

Peter, a disciple of Jesus, denied that he even knew Him in a moment of crisis, a mistake that led to deep discouragement and self-loathing. Imagine how disgusted and disappointed Peter must've been with himself. He had walked alongside Jesus, watching Him teach, watching Him perform miracles to heal people, watching Him raise the dead, watching Him offer mercy and forgiveness over and over again. Yet the first time he was put to the test and confronted about his commitment to Jesus, he denied Him three times.

Instead of ignoring or rationalizing the mistake, Peter did the right thing. He was humble and regretful. He didn't drift into despair. He didn't waste time suffering in condemnation. He owned up to his mistake and grieved. Peter cast all his anxiety on God, and his life was filled with renewed hope because of God's mercy. That was the key to Peter's healing.

"Never be defined by your past mistakes. It was just a lesson, not a life sentence." — Rick Warren

---

After the resurrection of Jesus, the two met again on the seashore. Jesus reminded Peter of how much good could come from his awful betrayal. Three times Jesus asked Peter: "Do you love me?" (John 21:17). He was giving Peter the opportunity to make up for the three times he had denied Jesus, which was obviously a gigantic mistake.

It would've been easy for Peter to isolate himself, to pretend that he hadn't made such a serious mistake. But deep down, he knew he wasn't meant to go through life on his own. He knew we are all better together—that we're meant for a shared community.

Some of the great people in the Bible made very poor choices. The apostle Paul started off as a murderer, yet his destiny was bigger than his mistakes. He ended up becoming a great leader and writing over half of the New Testament. Our mistakes, our failures, our poor choices don't have to keep us from our God-given destiny. With God, it's not about the way you start in life—it's about the way we finish.

If you are in a pit, dealing with enormous adversity, understand that God knows everything. He knows what you're dealing with down to the last detail. And He can play an integral role in the results, but your faith must endure. You need to honor Him by trusting Him even if it seems as though He is ignoring you. He has a purpose for your life and will not let you suffer anything that doesn't serve that purpose.

When we are going through pain, nonbelievers are watching us, wondering what it means to be a Christian suffering the same kind of pain they are. The truth is our successes don't give us credibility; our suffering does. So, the more honest and vulnerable you are about the suffering in your life, the more powerful your impact will be in people's lives.

If you have a problem, there is nothing wrong with saying, "Lord, I am hurting, and I need You." You don't have to go it alone. When problems prompt us to pray, they actually do more good than harm. The Bible tells us you can take whatever is currently weighing you down and bring that load to Jesus. Just remember, God's response might happen on His timeline, not yours, and His response isn't always to fix your problems. He might want to fix *you* first. We do not mature spiritually overnight. We must learn perseverance, and that means believing God is working in our lives, even if we don't feel it at the moment.

We must view ourselves as God views us: favorable, loved, wanted, and needed. In times of adversity, I have learned to make my first step toward a solution a step toward the Lord, going before Him just as David did. God longs to hear your words. Your honest and forthright declaration is precisely what prayer is all about.

We must learn to deal with both the good and the bad in life. We all need to be more resolute and not so quick to give up when things seem hard. And sometimes learning to deal with the good is actually the hardest thing of all.

Serving Comes Back Around

Another strategy I've learned for dealing with adversity is helping other people. You will get God's attention if you are still helping others in your time of need. The love and goodness you spread in the world will all come back to you in the form of blessings, even if you don't recognize them at first.

Focus on your purposes and not your problems. If you focus on your problems, you'll head down the rabbit hole of self-centeredness where there is only your problem, your issue, and your pain. If you focus on your purpose, your attention will turn to God and helping others.

Maybe you've had a setback in life. Maybe you've done something you regret, bailed on a commitment you made, or had a lapse of faith. Know this: your setback can turn out to be a setup. Your test can become your testimony. You don't have to be controlled or crippled by your past.

If you are worn out and exhausted from your past mistakes, if you are filled with sadness and depression, there is hope. But this hope is not in religion or in rules or regulations. It is the hope of Jesus Christ coming to live inside of you.

There is no shortcut to recovering from mistakes. The greater the failure, the more time it takes to heal. And the most important thing you can do after experiencing failure is to cast yourself at God's mercy. Let God inside; let God work in your heart. When you repent of your mistakes, God always offers another chance. But you must reach out to Him so you can face the world and the future again with courage and hope.

Make it your goal to spend time with God every day. Pick a time and a place where you are less likely to be interrupted. Talk to

God about the important things in your life. Read His Word and consider what it means for your life.

After all these years of hustling and grinding, here is what I've learned about problems:

- We all fail. Don't throw away your problems. You can learn from them.
- Don't let your problems make you bitter. Let your problems make you better.
- Some problems are more triumphant than victories.
- You must have long-range goals to keep from being frustrated by short-term problems.
- Someone who makes a mistake and doesn't correct that mistake is making yet another problem.
- Staying calm is the key to overcoming problems.

As I've gained wisdom through God and His words, I find my mistakes are becoming smaller in scale. That's progress. Most of the successful people I've met in the business, sports, and entertainment worlds have all consistently failed before reaching their true potential. But if you learn from your mistakes, they might not be mistakes at all.

Jesus is in the business of giving people a fresh start. And no matter how much you've messed up, you don't have to stay the same! When you confess your mess to Jesus, He lovingly and graciously responds by giving you a fresh start.

God wants you to ask for help when you are in trouble. He is telling you to call on Him when you need help so you can be sure that He will hear you. Your God is the one who saves you and rescues you when you need it.

Honestly, sometimes we don't want to be helped. We are convinced that we know what's best as if we are more qualified than God. At other times, we are too embarrassed to ask God for help. We feel like we're not good enough to deserve help, so we let our guilt keep us from God.

Neither of these reasons are valid. We aren't more qualified than God, and His love for us is unconditional. God's help is the best help, and He offers it to you no matter what you've done!

When we call on God for help and He rescues us, the natural response is to honor God. If you want to honor God more with your life, ask for more of His help! When you make it a habit to ask God for help, you will honor Him more and more.

Keep in mind also that our thoughts are powerful. For example, maybe you believed the lie when someone said, "You are worthless. You don't matter." If you accepted that thought, even though it wasn't true, it shaped your life. Your thoughts determine your feelings, and your feelings determine your actions. To change your life, change your thoughts.

To change your life, change your thoughts.

Adversity will come at some time to everyone. No one I know personally or know of has ever experienced one success after another without defeats, failures, disappointments, and frustrations along the way. Learning to overcome them is what grows us up into maturity.

Great souls are grown through struggles, storms, and seasons of suffering. Be patient with the process. Allow the source of your frustration to do its work in your life.

And when problems arise, remember: God wants us to trust Him in times of trouble so He can rescue us—and we can give Him all the glory.

SCRIPTURE FOR FACING PROBLEMS

"Whoever conceals their sins does not prosper, but the one who confesses and renounces them finds mercy." (Proverbs 28:13)

"Listen to advice and accept discipline, and at the end you will be counted among the wise." (Proverbs 19:20)

"There is no one on earth who is righteous, no one who does what is right and never sins." (Ecclesiastes 7:20)

"I will forgive their wickedness and will remember their sins no more." (Jeremiah 31:34)

"Do everything without grumbling or arguing, so that you may become blameless and pure." (Philippians 2:14–15)

CHAPTER 10

WHY I CAN LACK PATIENCE

"The famous American prayer is, 'Dear God:
I pray for patience and I want it NOW!'"

I needed patience when I was having lunch in Phoenix with NBA superstar Kevin Garnett of the Minnesota Timberwolves after he signed a multimillion-dollar contract at the age of nineteen. The purpose of the luncheon was to share with Kevin a life insurance program, which offered some excellent savings for him. The challenge I had was being patient with Kevin, who had a difficult time taking off his headphones during our visit while he ordered three hot fudge sundaes for lunch. In the end, Kevin became a client, and I always admired his competitiveness on the court.

"Be patient with each other, making allowance for each other's faults because of your love." — Ephesians 4:2 NLT

When the Ground Shifts

But one important thing you need to remember is you are always going to be a work in progress. You will be growing and learning and messing up and relearning and growing for your entire life. Now, don't take that as an excuse to just quit trying. It's an opportunity that I hope you'll understand more by the time you finish this book.

"Time is one of God's most effective tools for teaching us to rely on Him." — Charles Stanley

---

Rushing In

It's not easy to wait on God. Instead, we rush and push. We jump in with both feet without looking first. As a result, we get overcommitted and fill our lives with the wrong things. We think we know what is best even though we don't have the full picture, but we try to control everything in our lives anyway. We think we can handle things better than God because He isn't doing things in the way and on the schedule we think is needed.

"Two things define you: your patience when you have nothing and your attitude when you have everything." — George Bernard Shaw

If you try to rush through the learning and growing part of the process, you may have to relearn lessons. If you didn't take the time and have patience with yourself to learn them fully the first time, you'll end up with a setback. It's like when I was in college and we got the questions for the test ahead of time. All I did was memorize the answers for that test. I didn't actually learn the material, so I couldn't tell you a week later what that class was all about. Had I needed that knowledge for my future job, I would have had to learn it all over again.

"Never discourage anyone who continually makes progress, no matter how slow." — Plato

During trials, we tend to take our eyes off the Lord and instead see only our problems. The longer we look at our circumstance, the larger the problems seem. When you feel that urgency to rush or the frustration of wanting to give up bubbling up inside of you, it's time to turn to God.

"No matter what storm you face, you need
to know that God loves you. He has not
abandoned you." — Benjamin Franklin

Find Your Source of Peace

One of life's frustrations is that God's timetable is rarely the same as yours. You are often in a hurry when God isn't, and you get frustrated with the seemingly slow progress you are making. I have heard there are two things that define a person: your patience when you have nothing, and your attitude when you do.

"People don't care about how much you
know until they know how much you
care." — President Theodore Roosevelt

Please believe me and take this to heart: You will get through whatever trial you're facing right now. Soon enough you will marvel at all that God did amid your trouble as you look back at it from the other side.

CHAPTER 11

WHY I NEED TO SHARE THE GOSPEL

"The best evangelist ever was Jesus.
The second best was Paul."

*W*alter Scott introduced me to Warren Buffett in Omaha. I had a good visit with Warren when I sat next to him at one of David Foster's charity dinners in Calgary, Canada. When we got better acquainted, I sent him one of Shaq's basketball shoes, size 23; he displays it along with Mark Maguire's baseball bat, which Mark had autographed for me and that I sent to Warren. (He's a big sports fan.)

One of Warren's quotes I like is, "You should be doing things that change lots of lives." That's exactly why I like to share the gospel. Perhaps 2 Corinthians 5:17 best sums everything up. Paul wrote, "If anyone is in Christ, the new creation has come: The old has gone, the new is here!" In other words, when you put your trust in Christ, regardless of your past, you become a brand-new person—and you can't help but share about the change with others who are looking for hope and healing as well.

"You are the only Bible some nonbelievers will ever read." — John MacArthur

---

In 1975, I had a life insurance appointment with superstar speaker and legendary trainer Tom Hopkins at a restaurant in Phoenix. Tom wrote eighteen books, some of which sold millions of copies.

I had all my insurance sales material ready for my business meeting with Tom. I was hoping he would become a client by buying a life insurance policy. When I started getting acquainted with Tom at lunch, I could see the void in his life and where he was empty in many areas, even though he was very successful. I immediately put my insurance material to the side, and I shared what the Bible says on how to be saved. At the luncheon, he did not become a life insurance client, but more importantly, he prayed with me to receive Jesus as his Lord and Savior.

Within a short period of time at Tom's seminars, he would give attendees an opportunity to hear how his life changed by receiving Christ. He announced that this was purely optional since it was not part of his seminar program, but many attended, and Tom led others to the Lord by giving his testimony.

Magic Johnson and Isaiah Thomas told me that Pete Maravich created Showtime in the NBA. Before that, at Louisiana State University in 1966–67, "Pistol Pete" had averaged 44.9 points per game, with a total of 3,687 points, which remained the most points scored in a Division 1 basketball career until Caitlin Clark broke the record in 2024.

I met Pete through Paul Westphal, an all-star from the Phoenix Suns. Pete spoke in our home at one of our dinner parties, sharing that even with all of his basketball success, his life was a total mess and there were times he even considered suicide. In 1984, Pistol Pete had signed what was at the time the largest basketball contract ever, $800,000 with the Atlanta Hawks. He said even all that money did not fulfill him and admitted he was empty until he received Jesus as his Savior.

Pete told me many times that God is not a good God, He is a *great* God! He had a wonderful testimony, and he often spoke at Billy Graham's rallies. Pete was always interested in leading people to Jesus.

Pete died suddenly in 1988, at age forty, during a pickup basketball game at a Nazarene church playing with Focus on the Family founder Dr. James Dobson. Pete, it turned out, had an undetected heart defect—but the true heart of who he was would live on into eternity because of his faith and trust in his Lord and Savior.

Russell Sigler was not quite that young—he was ninety-five when he agreed to have lunch with me, where the conversation was predetermined: we were going to talk about heaven. Sigler was a legendary businessman. He served throughout the Pacific Theater in World War II and retired from the military as a lieutenant colonel in 1946. He studied under Willis Carrier, the founder of modern-day air conditioning. He started his own business with $15,000 in savings bonds he had sent home to his parents.

In 1949, he wrote himself a note, stating his expectations of having $1 million by 1980. He was going to accomplish this by building an air conditioning empire, which is exactly what he did.

At lunch, I asked Russ the following questions:

Would you agree that life is very short and temporary?

Is your faith important to you?

Do you believe in prayer?

Do you believe in the Bible?

Do you think about heaven?

Do you believe in heaven?

To each query, he responded quickly and in the affirmative.

Then I asked him if he was 100 percent sure he was going to heaven. He said he wasn't.

I shared several scriptures, starting with John 3:16: "For God so loved the world [and Russ] that he gave his one and only Son, that whoever believes in him shall not perish but have eternal life."

I shared with Russ that none of us are perfect, for all have sinned and fallen short of the glory of God (Romans 3:23). I shared that Jesus died on the cross for our sins, having proclaimed that He was "the way and the truth and the life" (John 14:6). And that's when Russ, ninety-five, prayed with me to receive Jesus Christ as his Lord and Savior, inviting Him into his life.

From that point on, Russ was never ashamed of the gospel. He was willing to share with others his newborn faith, proving it is never too late to receive Jesus as your Savior. Russ waited until he was ninety-five to make the most important decision in his life, but you don't have to! You can say yes to Jesus and place your faith in Him *today*, and then watch as He begins to transform your life from the inside out.

As any Christian knows, witnessing is not easy. It can be a minefield. But it is desired by God. It is the act of publicly professing one's devotion to Christ and claiming Him fully. It's informing others about Jesus and all He has done for the world.

You never know who is going to be offended by the mere mention of God. Once, I was in the back seat of a cab heading to the airport in Washington, DC, enjoying a very nice conversation with a very engaging driver. But when I mentioned Jesus, the man turned around and screamed at me: "If you ever mention the name *Jesus* again I am going to kick you out of this cab!"

You should never force Jesus upon the unwilling, but sometimes you have to risk making someone else uncomfortable. Procrastination and the word *tomorrow* have kept far too many people out of heaven.

And the eighteen inches between one's head and one's heart is a longer journey than you might imagine—one that often is never completed. Many people know about God in their heads but refuse to welcome Him into their hearts. They will forever remain eighteen inches from heaven, and to me, that's a shame.

Some people simply won't give God a chance. They won't receive the gospel you are trying to share no matter how compelling your argument. Their minds are made up and they are not willing to listen. The tragedy of a closed mind and a hard heart is that even if a little seed gets through, it can't grow because it can't take root. But that doesn't mean we shouldn't try.

Why We Are Called to Witness

There have been many times in my life when I have been afraid of sharing Christ with someone. The biggest reason is always the fear of rejection. And there are occasions when I have pulled back and kept my distance. The fear of disapproval always comes from a hidden wound. However, when I feel led by the Holy Spirit, knowing how God has accepted me and understands my motives, nothing gets in my way. Why? Because we are instructed in the Bible to spread the Word, and, frankly, most of us don't follow this particular command.

"The meaning of life is to find your gift. The purpose of life is to give it away." — Pablo Picasso

---

The gospel is meant to be shared, not hidden. Imagine being a doctor. You're introduced to someone with a life-threatening illness and you know how to treat it but refuse to say anything. Maybe you say nothing because you feel uncomfortable talking to people or because you think they won't want to hear what you have to say. Would you really hold back from sharing something that could save their life just because you were uncomfortable? The same is true about sharing the gospel.

I do not believe evangelism is imposing anything on anyone; it is simply telling the truth. I also believe Satan does not want us to introduce people to Jesus. It's a fact that many Christians feel uptight when they evangelize. However, I believe many of our friends want to be saved; they just don't know the truth of God's love. And God doesn't want anyone lost. That is why He commanded us to go and spread the Word.

The Bible is clear on God's instruction about witnessing. God is looking for us to say, "Use me Lord. I will go where You want me to go. I will say what You want me to say."

We can't be ashamed of the gospel if we understand what it did for us in this life and for eternity. When you're sharing your faith with others, there's power in your personal story about how accepting Jesus and the decision to walk in faith has changed your life. You just need to be willing to share it.

As Christians, we should ask ourselves, What am I doing for the Lord? When was the last time I shared the gospel with someone? If Jesus tells us to go and make disciples of all nations (Matthew 28:19), why am I not obeying Him?

The reality is most people don't really know what they believe. They may label themselves as Christians or atheists or Muslims. But when you scratch beneath the surface, they sometimes have no idea what their belief system entails.

"Be kind, for everyone you meet is fighting a hard battle." — Plato

---

The most controversial scripture in the Bible is probably John 14:6—one of the verses I shared with Russ, where Jesus says, "I am the way and the truth and the life. No one comes to the Father except through me." Traditionally, this has been interpreted to claim that Christianity is the only religion that leads to God. Whenever someone argues that such a statement is narrow-minded and exclusive, my comment is that I did not say it; Jesus did. I could have let fear prevent me from being direct with my friend, but then I wouldn't have had the privilege of seeing him accept Jesus into his heart and lead others to the Lord.

You may not want to witness because you don't want to offend people. Remember, no matter what you do in life, somebody's not going to like it. You can't avoid disapproval. So, if you're going to have people's disapproval either way, you may as well have it for doing the right thing rather than the wrong thing. This is important to remember as you face opposition. If someone else's opinion matters more to you than God's opinion, then you're going to crumble when people attack you because of your faith in Jesus.

But if you focus on God and what you know is right, then you can make a firm stand.

What's in It for You—and for Them?

The most important thing to remember when inviting others on the journey of faith you are taking is what it does for them. But it's also good to remember what is in it for you. Even if you feel unequipped or clumsy in how you share your faith, it's important to try.

When you get to heaven, God will ask you, "What did you do with what I gave you? Did you use it to serve others? Did you go everywhere in the world and tell the good news to everyone?" (See Mark 16:15.)

"The Holy Spirit will move nonbelievers by first moving you. If you can rest without them being saved, they will rest, too. But if you are filled with an agony for them, if you cannot bear that they should be lost, you will soon find that they are uneasy, too." — Charles Spurgeon

---

You may not win a popularity contest by sharing the plan of salvation with others, but you will certainly gain the favor of your Father in heaven. And that's not all. You will have the assurance that death is only temporary separation from your loved ones and that you will be with them again in eternity. Pastor Rick Warren said it best: "Imagine how good you will feel when you meet someone in heaven, and they thank you for them being there. Helping people get into heaven is the greatest act of mercy you can do for them." And as you can see from Russ's story, it's never too late.

It's common to get anticipatory fear. You might experience trepidation and anxiety over how to get the conversation rolling. But Luke 21:13–15 tells us about God's promise to help us through it: "And so you will bear testimony to me. But make up your mind not to worry beforehand how you will defend yourselves. For I will give you words and wisdom that none of your adversaries will be able to resist or contradict." You may not feel ready or equipped to share the gospel, but you have everything you need in God's presence, with His power inside of you. That should give you a lot of comfort in your message.

To grow as Christians we need to remain focused on three key areas: to pray more, to read the Bible daily, and to introduce people to Jesus. I have an insatiable hunger to lead people to Christ. I want to be remembered as an evangelist Christian. The three most important words in my life are "God, use me." Christianity isn't like a product that works for some and not for others. Christianity, simplified, is a relationship with Christ Himself. That is why we need to get over our fear about sharing our faith.

Remember, there are people all around you who need to hear about Jesus Christ. Whether it's someone in your neighborhood, at the office, or in your own family, bringing them into the family of God is the greatest thing you can do. The best place to learn how is in your church family. Will you take a step of faith and start an evangelistic conversation?

How to Witness

There are plenty of pamphlets, instructions in church, and other guidance for what to say and how to present the plan of salvation, but I believe the two most powerful and effective ways to share your faith are through your words and your actions.

People listen to what you say and then watch what you do when you profess to be a Christian, so it is important to make sure they line up with each other.

Marvin Lewis is a former NFL head coach who led the Cincinnati Bengals to the playoffs more times than not. He was the 2009 NFL Coach of the Year, and he is a permanent fixture at the chapel. He strongly believes in one-on-one time with the chaplain as well as group Bible studies. And he found an ingenious method to witness. He didn't give his players a choice! "I'll basically mandate that everyone goes to chapel at least once because I want them to have the experience of it," Lewis said.

You may not have the same kind of influence Marvin does, but you can be consistent in your example wherever you are and take every opportunity God presents to you to share the gospel.

"We make a living by what we get. We make a life by what we give." — Winston Churchill

---

You see, inviting others on the journey of faith isn't just about sharing the plan of salvation and talking to people about Jesus and how to get to heaven. We are representatives of God to the world, and what we say on other matters, and how we say it, speaks volumes too. Make sure that what you are adding to the words God gives you aligns with His message.

If you were to ask fifty random people, "How do you get to heaven?" you'd get close to fifty different answers. You'd hear things like, "Do more good things than bad things in life" or "Be a religious person." Many of their answers would be based on working to please God instead of resting in His grace. Salvation is a gift from God. It's absolutely free! You can't earn it or buy it. You can only receive it in faith.

You don't get to heaven based on what you do. You get to heaven based on what has already been done for you by Jesus Christ! Praise God for His gracious gift!

If you knew, with certainty, that you were going to die tomorrow, what would your prayers look like tonight?

One day your heart will stop beating, and that will be the end of your body.

But your life doesn't end with death.

You were made in God's image, which means you were designed to last forever. Death is just a transition into eternal life with God or eternal life without God. For Christians, death is not leaving home; it's a homecoming.

Hope That Does Not Disappoint

We have this hope because of our faith in Christ. God is the God of hope, and it is a hope that will not disappoint. We believe in the hope of the resurrection because the same power that resurrected Jesus will resurrect you.

You will encounter many doors in your life: doors to happiness, doors to sadness, doors to success, and doors to failure.

Your success in life largely depends on which doors you decide to walk through. But there is one door you just can't afford to miss: the door to salvation. Your salvation is important to God. He wants you to live free in Christ. Jesus saves you for eternity and from your problems.

As a believer, you don't need to live in fear or worry. God doesn't want you to wonder whether or not you will be in heaven with Him. God does not want you to doubt your salvation.

The apostle John made it clear: If you believe in Jesus, you can know for certain that you have eternal life. In this life, God doesn't answer every one of your questions. But the question about eternal security is answered with a resounding "Yes!"

When we die, our physical bodies will decay, but our souls will enter the afterlife. Those who have put their faith in Jesus Christ will immediately go into the presence of God. The Bible says, "And this world is fading away, and these evil, forbidden things will go with it, but whoever keeps doing the will of God will live forever" (1 John 2:17 TLB).

Jesus said, "I am the resurrection and the life. The one who believes in me will live, even though they die; and whoever lives by believing in me will never die" (John 11:25–26).

Evangelism is every day in every way helping your nonbelieving friends to take one step closer to Jesus Christ.

I think one of the most important things we can do as Christians is to learn to become heavenly-minded. We have all heard the expression, "They're so heavenly-minded, they're no earthly good," but the fact is, people who are truly heavenly-minded do the most earthly good.

The Bible actually tells us in Colossians 3:2 to "set your minds on things above." You could translate it this way: "Think about heaven." It's a good thing to be heavenly-minded—to contemplate and consider heaven.

We cannot force someone to hear a message they are not ready to receive. But we must never underestimate the power of planting a seed.

Today is the day of salvation. Soon it will be too late.

SCRIPTURE FOR INVITING OTHERS ON THE JOURNEY

"Lord, help me to realize how brief my time on earth will be." (Psalm 39:4 TLB)

———

"And you will be my witnesses, telling people about me everywhere." (Acts 1:7-8 NLT)

———

"Go and make disciples of all nations." (Matthew 28:19)

———

"What good will it be for someone to gain the whole world, yet forfeit their soul?" (Matthew 16:26)

———

"Come, follow me, and I will show you how to fish for people!" (Matthew 4:19 NLT)

CHAPTER 12

WHY I WANT TO
BE SUCCESSFUL

"The only place success comes before
work is in the dictionary."

*I*t is no secret that success as measured by money doesn't always bring happiness.

A good example of someone who is very successful financially but who lives his life by giving back to the less fortunate is Andrea Bocelli, considered by many to have the best voice in the world.

I met Andrea in an elevator at the Ritz-Carlton in New York. Andrea immediately told me that his hero was Muhammad Ali, and after I was able to make the introduction with him and the Champ, Andrea and I became very good friends and have done numerous charity events together with our foundations in Italy.

The Andrea Bocelli Foundation helps those in poverty, illiteracy, and distress due to illness and social exclusion. Andrea is inspired to help young people, and a good example would be the five schools he and his wife, Veronica, built in Haiti.

Perhaps the message of Luke 12:48 best describes Andrea: to whom much is given, much is expected.

Many people in this world label success as living in a large home, driving nice cars, and boasting a high net worth. But I know many people who are wealthy and have plenty, and some of them will admit they are very empty on the inside.

Jerry Colangelo is an exception. He is the godfather of Arizona sports. He once owned the Phoenix Suns. He brought the Diamondbacks to Arizona, a new franchise that won a World Series in its fourth year. He brought the NHL to the Valley, relocating the Winnipeg Jets. And he is largely responsible for the stunning growth of downtown Phoenix.

Colangelo has been a very important influence on my life because he has never lost sight of the big picture. He will tell you that his top priorities are, in order, God, family, work, and the many charities he supports. And over the course of a friendship that has spanned fifty-plus years, he's helped me keep my priorities straight as well.

"If people knew how hard I had to work to gain my mastery, it would not seem so wonderful at all..." — Michelangelo

---

For a legitimate sports icon, Colangelo has retained a great sense of humility that I also try to emulate.

Let Your Light Shine

Pete Maravich's favorite scripture, he would tell me, was Matthew 5:16, "Let your light shine before others, that they may see your good deeds and glorify your Father in heaven." This scripture does a good job of describing my close friend Jerry Colangelo, who has been a very important influence in my life when it comes to priorities.

I know I sound judgmental, but when I see some of these professional athletes making millions of dollars and broadcasting their $50 million homes and expensive cars and multimillion-dollar yachts on Facebook, it turns me off.

I will tell you what turns me on: successful, professional athletes who have handled their success with humility. I have done business with Pete Sampras, the number-one player in the world in tennis during his era, and I had floor seats for him at the Phoenix Suns game. Pete told me he preferred not to sit on the floor since he didn't want the attention.

Wayne Gretzky told me that hockey star Shane Doan is the nicest person he's ever met. Why? Because Shane is humble and thinks first of other people instead of himself, even though he's one of the greatest professional hockey players ever.

Should you ask Billy Jean King, Chris Evert, or Jimmy Connors about what they think of Wimbledon champion Stan Smith, they would agree that Stan is one of the nicest guys ever to play tennis. Stan has always been very humble and is well known for being a respected Christian. He gave his testimony in our backyard at a dinner party before 150 people, and many invited Jesus into their life when he shared his story.

There are many other examples of humble athletes I could share, but I will finish with this story. Charles Barkley and Julius Erving will tell you that their Philadelphia 76ers teammate Bobby Jones was not only humble but a Christian man they highly admired. The owner of the Sixers, Harold Katz, told me when they were in a close game in the fourth quarter, Bobby was coming across midcourt and yelled to Barkley and Erving, "If you guys will quit your cussing, I think we can win this game!" Everyone loved Bobby, who was a great competitor and always put his team ahead of his own personal accomplishments.

When people say kind things about me, that's when I'll mention that I don't want to appear to be a Christian who has a perfect life. I struggle, and I have fallen more times than I would like to admit. That's why I need Jesus. I can relate to Proverbs 24:16: "Though the righteous fall seven times, they rise again."

Don't get me wrong; success is not a bad thing. Everyone wants to succeed. Whether it's in a game or in business, I want to win. I have a passion to be successful, and I have been blessed beyond my wildest dreams.

I've also learned a very important lesson along the way: People define success differently based on their own priorities, their age, their sense of purpose, and the expectations of family, peers, and society. In America, success is usually defined by money, power, and fame. And unfortunately, we can easily fall into the trap of chasing that dream rather than what really is fulfilling for us. Being successful in worldly terms is not the ultimate victory in life.

The first step toward that victory is to ask yourself how you define success.

What Is Success?

I am someone who works hard and loves hard work, but I don't want to be known as a workaholic. Still, I know successful people don't happen by accident. They have passion, ambition, and drive. They have focus, vision, and stamina. They have a strong work ethic. They set goals. They create a plan to achieve those goals. And then they execute the plan to its fruition.

"Do not judge me by my successes. Judge me by how
many times I fell down and got back up again."
— former president of South Africa Nelson Mandela

But how did they learn to do that in the first place? Some
people are just born with that drive. Others have to get there by
trial and error. Part of that trial and error is figuring out what
success means to you and deciding if that is a realistic perspective
or if it is based on the opinions of other people who shouldn't have
influence over you.

How the World Defines It

It's very easy to get attached to idols. Sometimes they are unhealthy
standards we hold up as the goal, but often they are just good
things that we adore in an inappropriate way or to an unwarranted level. And idols are everywhere in our society. They come
in the form of musicians, actors, or people who don't do anything
special but are very attractive, and they come in the form of money,
possessions, influence, or power.

Keep in mind that these things are not inherently evil. It's okay
to admire someone who creates something you enjoy or are moved
by. There is nothing wrong with wanting to have nice things and
financial security. It's even appropriate to desire power and influence when it is used to make people's lives better. The problem
comes when our longing for these things leads to obsession over
them or putting them on a pedestal.

The PBS documentary *Affluenza* is a groundbreaking film
from 1997 that "diagnoses a serious social disease caused by

consumerism, commercialism and rampant materialism." The program claimed that

- the average American shops six hours a week while spending forty minutes playing with their children;
- by age twenty, we've seen one million commercials; and
- in 90 percent of divorce cases, arguments about money play a prominent role.[2]

And of course, those factors have become even more prevalent in our internet and digital age. What struck me about the program is that it didn't argue against materialism on a moral basis but a pragmatic one: material wealth doesn't make us happy.

"The difference between successful and unsuccessful people is that successful people do a lot of the things that unsuccessful people don't want to do."
— Self-made billionaire and
philanthropist John Paul DeJoria

In a similar way, many unfortunate lottery winners discover they are not prepared to handle the demands of great wealth. They typically splurge it all away, fall prey to the unwise investment schemes of family and friends, and succumb to the relentless appeals of charities. Many have even committed suicide. This is proof that money and all it can buy are not the keys to success, no matter what the world tells you.

What Success Really Is

Success isn't a clear-cut benchmark you achieve. For one person, it might be rising to CEO of their company; for another it might be having their own company where they work from home. Success could be having the freedom to travel the world, or it could be having a big family and staying in your small hometown. Success is not determined by reaching a certain net worth or getting a specific number of social media followers. If that is your proof of success, then it will never be stable. It can easily go back in the other direction. That sense of joy is elusive.

John D. Rockefeller was one of the wealthiest men who ever lived. He was once asked, How much is enough? "Just a little more," he said. Rockefeller eventually discovered the truth. He said, "I have made many millions of dollars, but they have brought me no happiness." After his death, someone asked Rockefeller's accountant how much money he had left behind. The answer was an instant classic.

"He left . . . all of it," the accountant said.

You have to ask yourself: Am I going to live for possessions? Popularity? Am I going to be driven by external pressures? Guilt? Bitterness? Materialism? Or am I going to be led by God's purpose for my life?

I have learned that if I allow success to be used only in a self-gratifying way, I will lack purpose. The secret to success remains the same throughout the Bible. It's the presence of God. When we devote our lives to Him, success naturally follows.

"If you need something done, you ask a busy person to do it." — Renowned neurosurgeon Dr. Ben Carson

---

Significance is about others—loving and serving people. One of the greatest questions we can ask ourselves is, *Does my life change other people's lives for the better?* We all win when putting others first.

How Do You Achieve Success?

In his book *Halftime: Moving from Success to Significance,* Bob Buford writes that at some point in your life, it's important to pause and consider how to make the transition to living your ideal life. Buford says that visualizing where you want to be, what you want to be doing, and who you would like to be doing it with are keys to living an ideal life.

I was once asked to speak to honor students at Arizona State University, and one of the subjects I focused on was the importance of choosing your friends carefully. What kind of person do you want to become in ten years? The people you spend time with will largely determine your future. You become like the people closest to you.

Show me a flourishing enterprise in any walk of life, and at the very top, I'm betting you'll find a determined, disciplined, dynamic leader who understands there are no elevators waiting to whisk you to the top. You have to take the stairs.

Successful people are willing to do whatever it takes, including the things that unsuccessful people don't feel like doing. They develop good habits and stay committed. They are ordinary people with extraordinary determination.

I've always been a planner. I'm a fanatic about jotting down ideas and things to do on anything within my reach—pieces of newspaper, napkins, the backs of business cards—or methodically posting them into my handheld electronic organizer.

Strength of conviction is also a key to success. You must believe in yourself because you are your own best champion. Plug into your passion and powerful things happen.

Here are some other success-fostering tips:

- Act as if you belong, no matter where you are. Combine networking with one of your passions, which will make networking much easier for you.
- Follow the Golden Rule: treat others as you wish to be treated.
- Stay persistent. Never be afraid to introduce yourself first.
- Be a great listener and ask open-ended questions. Remember, God gave you two ears and one mouth, so use them in proportion.
- No matter how you are feeling in the morning, adopt the following mantra: "Get up, dress up, show up, and never give up."
- Do everything with integrity, even when no one is watching.

What Are the Barriers to Success?

One thing is certain: If you take away conviction, discipline, and determination, you have cut the heart out of a meaningful life. You have eliminated the challenge that keeps the game of life exciting and rewarding. You have erased the very things that made giants out of historic leaders such as General Patton, General MacArthur, Winston Churchill, Vince Lombardi, Tom Landry, and Ludwig von Beethoven.

"Success is a lousy teacher. It seduces smart people into thinking they can't lose." —Microsoft cofounder Bill Gates

---

Once attained, success can be fleeting, so it must be sustained with the same zeal and energy. Ask any professional sports team that has won a championship, and the players will tell you the same thing: it's easier to get to the top than to stay on top.

What God Says about Success

I've been blessed to meet so many famous professional athletes, entertainers, and businesspeople, but that has never given me even a fraction of the joy, the peace, and the value I have gained in knowing Jesus.

On your own, there is no guarantee that you will be successful at anything. But when you step out in faith, trusting God and pursuing His work for you, He guarantees your success.

Remember, God is more interested in us being faithful than being successful. You can reach the highest pinnacle in business, but if you don't have the Lord, it's not going to fulfill you. God wants us to prosper. However, God won't bless us if we're motivated by greed, guilt, selfishness, fear, or pride.

God is more interested in what you're becoming than in what's happening to you. He often allows trials, troubles, tribulations, and problems in your life to teach you diligence, determination, and character. The problem you're going through right now is a test of your faithfulness. Will you continue to serve God when the going gets tough?

We can do worse than fail. We can succeed and take all of the credit for our success. We can succeed and worship the accomplishment rather than the one who helped us reach it.

I believe you should figure out what you love to do, what God gave you a heart to do, and then do it for His glory. In the movie *Chariots of Fire*, Olympian Eric Liddell said, "I believe God made me for a purpose . . . and when I run, I feel His pleasure."

God gifted Liddell beyond his running ability. A year after winning his gold medal, he became a missionary in China. He didn't have any regrets leaving behind fame and fortune; he knew a life serving others counted far more than just running races. He understood that God gave him his gifts not to enrich himself but to serve others and share his faith. (And he died in China, an ultimate sacrifice for the gospel.) God blesses you so you can bless others.

Moses is a strong, biblical example of a man with many successful qualities. When Moses grew up, he refused to be known as the son of Pharaoh's daughter. By faith, he left Egypt, not fearing the king's anger and retribution. It was Moses' dream when he led two million Hebrews out of Egypt and into the promised land. During that time, people complained and argued. They did not have enough faith to enter the promised land, and they spent forty years wandering in the desert.

"If you want to make everybody happy, then don't be a leader; instead sell ice cream!"
— Apple cofounder and CEO Steve Jobs

Moses was mistreated by many as he was leading the Jews out of Egypt. He could've stayed in the lap of luxury, indulging in the sinful pleasures of Pharaoh's palace. But he didn't want to live his life for pleasure.

Moses was very mature. Even though he could have attained great power, he instead listened to God. He had great faith. He also knew popularity does not last long. Moses rejected temporary pleasure because he had his values and priorities right. He rejected material things because he knew there was something more important in this life.

The same can be true for us. If we live for happiness, we'll never find it. But if we instead channel our energy into being holy, we will be truly happy. Holy people are happy people because happiness is a fringe benefit of holiness.

Just like athletes who must train diligently to qualify for the Olympics, you don't become godly by simply doing what you feel like doing. Godly men and women choose to develop the habits that produce godliness in their lives. It's not any easier than working out or dieting or rehearsing or anything else that requires work. But the sacrifice is well worth the effort.

When you believe that you are valuable and worthy because of who lives inside you, everything changes. You find meaning. You discover purpose. Significance exists within each day. And when you soak in the truth that you were created in the image of God, by love, in love, and for love, you begin to see the world differently. You see people in a new light. Your eyes open to hurt, and your heart bleeds for those who are hurting. Your priorities shift and you begin to understand that it doesn't matter how successful you are—significance matters more. And significance is found when you align yourself with what matters to God and move forward each day.

On more than one occasion, the Bible uses the analogy of running a race. For the Christian, the race of life is knowing God and having a relationship with Him. But it isn't enough just to *run* the race. We have to *finish* the race we've begun, and that takes discipline.

Your Lord and Savior wants to occupy first place. Matthew 6:33 says that when you seek Him first, everything else "will be given to you as well." How long has it been since you've enlisted your Lord's help in a private, personal temple-cleansing session?

More Blessed in Giving

The Lord knows how to satisfy our hearts while meeting all our needs. Our greatest wealth is His blessing. And it's not just material needs He supplies. He takes care of us emotionally, spiritually, relationally, mentally, and eternally. A trillion dollars is nothing compared to a heart that trusts in God.

True happiness comes from service. God designed you to be happiest when you are giving your life away. Why? Because He wants you to become like Him, and He gave Himself away in love. It's all about love!

"Success comes in a lot of ways, but it doesn't come with money [or] fame. It comes from having a meaning in your life, doing what you love, and being passionate about [it]." — former NFL quarterback and Heisman Trophy winner Tim Tebow

---

To have a happy heart, you have to practice service and generosity every day. The Bible teaches us that there is more happiness in giving than in receiving (Acts 20:35). When I was a kid, I didn't believe that. I was immature and thought it was more fun to get than to give. And Christmas was always about me: "What am I going to get?" Later in life, I began to experience the joy that comes from giving. I slowly began to mature and understand there really is more joy in giving than in receiving.

Is your heart growing more generous every year? Are you more generous with your resources this year than you were a year ago?

Or are you stuck at the same level of generosity and wondering why you're also stuck in unhappiness?

Remember, God uses money to test us. Money shows what we love the most. But in the end, money means nothing if used only for personal possessions and material gain. It's about the journey and the lives we can touch, the legacy we can leave, and the world we can change for the better.

We all want to be successful, but motive is everything! Never forget your motive for serving—the "why" behind it all: It's all for Jesus. You owe your life to Him. The gratitude you have for what He lovingly did for you on the cross, knowing that one day you're going to stand before Him and hear Him say, "Well done, good and faithful servant" (Matthew 25:21)— that's what motivates you. It's not about making a name for yourself or always having fun.

If you want your life to turn from emptiness to overflowing, give Jesus complete control, including your career. We sometimes think, *God, if You'll make me really successful in business, then I'll serve You with the success.* Wrong! It's the exact opposite. We first give Jesus control, and then comes the success. That's the correct order.

"Using your time and talents to serve others—that's when truly meaningful success comes your way."
— Ken Blanchard, coauthor of *The One Minute Manager*

Remember how far you have come, not just how far you have to go. You may not be where you want to be, but you are also not where you used to be. God isn't finished with you, so keep moving forward.

In America, failure is almost an unpardonable sin, and we idolize success, but failure can be good for you. Failure doesn't have to be fatal. Wise people know how to take advantage of it. They accept it as one of God's primary tools in making them who He wants them to be.

God uses failure for a number of reasons, including

. . . **to educate you**. So take the opportunity to learn as much as you can. Mistakes are simply learning experiences, and some lessons can be learned only through failure. If you are not making any mistakes, you are not learning. If you are not taking any risks, you are not growing. When you are free from the fear of failure, you are free to grow.

. . . **to motivate you to change**. People don't change when they see the light; they change when they feel the heat. When you fail, maybe God's trying to get your attention to move you in a new direction.

. . . and **to build your character**. Failure has a way of softening your heart. It helps you grow and makes you sensitive to others. It makes you less judgmental and more sympathetic to people around you who are hurting. Yet failure doesn't automatically grow your character; it does so only when you respond to it correctly and learn from it.

"Whoever loves money never has enough." — Ecclesiastes 5:10

If you are wealthy and enjoy worldly success, you can hire someone to drive your car or make money for you, but you can't hire someone to stand in sick and die for you. Material things lost can be found again. But there is one thing that can never be found when it is lost: life.

Whatever our current stage of life, in time we will face the day the curtain closes. In light of that harsh but clarifying reality, we are wise if we focus our time and energy on loving God, our family, and our friends—treating them right and cherishing them.

As we get older and wiser we slowly realize that a $3,000 watch and a $30 watch both tell the same time. Whether the house we live in is 5,000 or 500 square feet, loneliness is the same. Therefore, I hope you realize, when you have friends and family with whom you can laugh, talk, sing, cry, rejoice, embrace, and love—this is the real happiness.

SCRIPTURE FOR SUCCESS

"Diligent hands will rule, but laziness ends in forced labor." (Proverbs 12:24)

———

"Take delight in the LORD, and he will give you the desires of your heart." (Psalm 37:4)

———

"A happy heart makes the face cheerful, but heartache crushes the spirit." (Proverbs 15:13)

———

"Commit to the LORD whatever you do, and he will establish your plans." (Proverbs 16:3)

CHAPTER 13

WHY I NEED MORE FAITH

"I have too many flaws in my life to be
perfect, but I have too many blessings
in my life not to be faithful."

Kurt Warner, a Hall of Fame quarterback who won two Most Valuable Player awards, led two of the worst franchises in NFL history to three different Super Bowls. As special and noteworthy as that was, my friend Kurt made a much bigger impact by selflessly living out the gospel of Jesus Christ to a member of my family in the wake of a deep disappointment.

In January 2000, Kurt caused quite a stir after the St. Louis Rams defeated the Tennessee Titans, 23–16, in Super Bowl XXXIV. "First things first," he said from the victory podium. "I've got to thank my Lord and Savior up above—thank you, Jesus!"

Warner received a lot of feedback for expressing his strong Christian beliefs on the biggest stage in professional sports. Much of it was unwarranted and unkind. But that's why many believe Warner to be a Hall of Fame *Christian*. He has never been ashamed of his faith. He doesn't just speak it; he models it through his action. I have been his friend for years and have seen it with my own eyes.

When my grandson Jonathon suffered an ACL injury before his senior season of football at Northern Arizona University, he was devastated that he could no longer play. I felt terrible, too, knowing how hard Jonathon had prepared for his final season in college.

I prayed for Jonathon, and almost immediately, Kurt's named popped into my head. I called him and explained the situation. Kurt responded by calling my grandson within five minutes. He spoke to Jonathon for thirty minutes, sharing some of his personal setbacks and disappointments.

Kurt is one of the greatest underdog stories in sports. He learned to trust God through his many adversities, and that's how he ended up a champion. He told my grandson that God has a plan for his life too. Shortly after they hung up, Jonathon called me.

"Papa!" he said. "Guess what? Kurt Warner just called me, and he really helped me with my disappointment!"

I was so touched. This was another example of how God has used a Christian man like Kurt Warner to serve and glorify Him.

Warner's pioneering spirit as a Christian athlete has broken down doors—and the main reason is because of how humbly he has represented and embodied his faith in Jesus.

Get Off Your High Horse

When I was growing up, my dad would often say, "Jimmy, get off your high horse." At the time, I thought he was telling me not to be conceited, cocky, or arrogant. But, looking back, I see his wisdom because what he was really telling me was, "Jimmy, be humble and good things will happen." Dad was right about that.

When I was in school at Arizona State, I knew all the good spots and hot clubs. I was a proud member of the Sigma Alpha Epsilon fraternity, in the middle of all the action. I had beach-blond hair, an oversize ego, and a Corvette convertible. I wasn't the humblest guy on campus.

Back then, Palm Springs, California, was an extremely popular spring break hot spot, even without a beach. I remember driving that Corvette with the top down, slowly cruising Palm Canyon Drive with girls sitting on the hood and on the back, eight girls in all.

> **"Being humble means recognizing that we are not on earth to see how important we can become, but to see how much difference we can make in the lives of others."** — Gordon B. Hinckley

I guess it really wasn't all that surprising when I noticed flashing red lights in my rearview mirror, along with the dreaded police siren signaling for me to pull over. I pretended to be surprised and asked the officer why he'd stopped me. I don't remember his response, although he quickly wrote me a ticket. Which I most definitely deserved. I was nowhere near the path of humility.

If I could speak today to a young Jimmy Walker, I would strongly caution him that no matter how smart or successful you are, nobody likes a braggart. No matter how good-looking or special you think you are, nobody likes arrogance. It took humiliation to teach me the virtue of humility.

My own arrogance and pride has often led me to think I am self-sufficient. When my health is good, when my bank account is full, when my friends are many and my name is well regarded, I tend to drift into complacency and forget I need to rely on God. It takes a lot of humility to rest and trust God when you're under attack, when you're misunderstood, and when people are spreading rumors about you. The impulse is to rise up and defend yourself, but that feeds your ego and edges God out, which is a step in the wrong direction.

I've had the privilege of knowing many other top athletes like Kurt Warner who have shown what it means to declare and demonstrate faith in our Savior.

Tony Dungy was the first African American coach in the NFL to win a Super Bowl, leading the Indianapolis Colts to victory in 2006. Tony has never been ashamed of sharing that winning isn't everything: Jesus is!

Tony is not only very vocal about his faith but he knows that if you follow Jesus, you *need* to take a stand for Him. Tony's faith is in God since he knows He has a purpose and a plan for everything we do in life.

Tony says our faith grows by spending time in prayer, and that is how we understand God's calling. Coach Dungy knows the Enemy will hit us where we are weakest and that his goal is to steal, kill, and destroy (John 10:10).

Another high-profile NFL pro who takes that stand is Brock Purdy, the young star quarterback for the San Francisco 49ers. He has one of the highest passing ratings in NFL history (in the company of greats like Aaron Rodgers and Patrick Mahomes), along with stellar completion and touchdown percentages.

But more important than talking football, Brock likes to talk about his Christian faith.

In 2019, when Purdy was still at Iowa State, he shared that he tried to use his football career to glorify God. "Every time I play—no matter what happens—I want others to see God through my actions. Every time I step on the field, I want to bring Him glory."

One of the scriptures on Purdy's mind throughout the NFL season is Mark 8:35, when Jesus called His disciples to pick up their cross and declared that "whoever wants to save their life will lose it, but whoever loses their life for me and for the gospel will save it."

"If you're trying to chase statues and money and all this kind of stuff, you'll lose your life, rather than denying yourself, picking up your cross, keeping your eyes on Jesus and His promises," Purdy said. "That's a life worth living, and that's how you save your life."

One of Purdy's fellow rising stars, C. J. Stroud of the Houston Texans, at age twenty-two is the youngest quarterback in NFL history to win a playoff game. In his rookie season he passed for over four thousand yards, which only a few NFL rookie quarterbacks have ever done.

Stroud has been vocal about his faith in Jesus Christ: "My foundation as a man is that I'm a man of God. I've been scarred and battle-tested, but I have the armor of God on me. My faith is very important to me."

Stroud led the Texans in the 2023–2024 season from one of the worst teams in the NFL to the playoffs. He constantly has credited all the glory for his success to Jesus Christ.

"Jesus laid His life on the cross for us—I really believe that. This is bigger than just football. Football is my platform. Spreading the gospel of Jesus Christ is my purpose. I think that's what God wants," Stroud asserted.

For too long, professional athletes were afraid of expressing their faith. They feared their words would be perceived as a sign of weakness. Kurt Warner's public declaration to Jesus helped to shift the mindset, as did Tony Dungy's. Today, a number of athletes show great courage and conviction in their faith.

Football attracts huge audiences and is a great platform for Christian athletes to express their love and faith in Jesus. But in the end, football is just a game.

The stakes were a lot higher for a lower-profile believer named Brother Andrew.

God's Smuggler

Andrew van der Bijl was known in the Christian world as "God's smuggler." He distributed over one million Bibles into Communist countries. Throughout his adult life, he snuck Bibles into places that would not approve of, much less appreciate, his efforts. He went behind the Iron Curtain and even smuggled Bibles into China.

Brother Andrew also traveled extensively in the Islamic world, talking to jihadists and leaders of Hamas and Hezbollah. He's among the few Western leaders who regularly journeyed to the Middle East as an ambassador for Christ. He was born in the Netherlands in 1928 and was still distributing Bibles when he died at age ninety-four in 2022.

The apostle Paul tells us to not be ashamed of the gospel (Romans 1:16). Brother Andrew followed that teaching as well as the instructions of Jesus, who told us to "go and make disciples of all nations" (Matthew 28:19). Brother Andrew proved that his faith was much stronger than his fear.

Sometimes that's easier said than done. We tend to have a problem trusting God, especially when the road gets rough and we feel we are alone or that our lives have too many hardships. That is normal and an expected part of being human. It's especially true as you begin your journey of walking in faith.

As detailed in the book of Exodus, Moses led the Israelites out of slavery in Egypt and eventually delivered them to the promised land. The journey should've taken only a few weeks, even with the logistical issues of transporting and leading hundreds of thousands of people. But it took them forty years. Why did their journey take so long? Because for forty years, the Israelites had a problem trusting God.

There was too much bickering and complaining. People lost their focus and their gratitude. They lost their faith, and they lost their way. I know a lot of people lose their faith following a personal tragedy such as the passing of a loved one. Since we can't avoid tragedies in life, how do we prevent a loss of faith during those times? Well, first we need to understand what is at the root of losing faith, and then we can know how to guard against it.

Losing Faith

Job from the Old Testament said, "I despise my life; I would not live forever. Leave me alone; my days have no meaning" (Job 7:16). Sometimes we get depressed and want to give up like Job did.

Storms come into our lives as Christians. Sometimes God will send the storm to test our faith, as in the case of Jonah, who was disobedient to God and effectively reaped the consequences of his actions. At other times, the devil will send a storm, and God will allow it. Sometimes we call on the Lord and He stops the storm. At other times He is with us and sustains us through the storm. But know this: Storms don't last forever. They have a beginning, a middle, and an end.

The Christian life is not a cakewalk. You are going to encounter struggles and times of doubt along the way. Becoming a Christian is not a guarantee of a trouble-free life. It's just a promise of a life full of hope and help.

Two of the biggest obstacles to keeping your faith are worry and fear. They make you question what you know to be true, and they keep you focused on the wrong things. Just like the Israelites in Egypt. They were worried that they had made matters worse by running, and they were afraid they wouldn't make it out alive. They lost their focus and forgot the promises God had made to them.

When we let fear and worry interfere with our thoughts, our faith can waver, and one of the most important things to learn as we take this journey is to grow in our faith so much that it can be tested by the struggles of life and hold up. Let's look at where fear and worry come from and how to combat them.

Restoring Faith

I don't like problems, but problems draw us to God. We need challenges in our lives so we can say, "God, I don't know how you are going to solve this problem, but by faith, my trust is in you." Faith in Christ will help us to deal with our problems.

God allowed Satan to bring a series of difficulties into Job's life. In one day, Job lost all of his children and all of his possessions. He had endured all he could handle, more than any human should be expected to suffer. And for a time, Job felt overwhelmed and wanted to give up. He even cursed the day he was born. But he held on, and his faith got him through the rough spots in the road.

When problems hit us, we apply the "Why?" test, which is the ultimate trial for our faith. When things don't make sense and we are searching for answers, we want to know why it happened, why we had to face this, why God didn't intervene. But in these moments, God is saying, "I'm right here beside you. Trust me. It may not be what you want, but it is what you need to go through to get where I want you to be."

We have talked about Moses and the difficulty he faced in getting the Israelites to trust God while they journeyed through the desert. But his faith was not shaken. Hebrews 11:27 (NLT) says, "It was by faith that Moses left the land of Egypt, not fearing the king's anger. He kept right on going because he kept his eyes on the one who is invisible."

How was he able to stay strong in his faith even though things looked hopeless? Because he grew his faith through his relationship with God.

Hebrews 11:1 provides an excellent definition: "Now faith is confidence in what we hope for and assurance about what we do not see." Faith isn't just a belief—it is belief put into action.

Growing Faith

How does faith grow? It can happen only if you make time in your schedule for God. Just as with our earthly relationships, our relationship with Him requires putting in effort and being in communication.

If I want to grow my relationship with my wife, Nancy, I have to spend time with her. I have to show her that I'm invested in getting to know her by making room in my schedule for her and making the time count. You cannot have a relationship with someone you never spend time with.

I also have to talk with her, hear what is on her mind, and share what is on mine. In a relationship with God, this means prayer. There are many ways to be more intentional about your prayer life, but it begins by making Him a priority. You can start a daily quiet time, getting alone with God to worship Him and learn from Him. You can keep a prayer journal of requests and answered prayer. God will speak to you and guide you if you just go to Him and ask for His help. (We talked much more about prayer in chapter 2.)

Prayer results in an indescribable and immediate sense of peace. That peace allows me to continue with what I need to do, in the confidence and assurance that God will work everything out. We were gutted when we lost our son, Scott, in 2019. I dove deeper into prayer, asking God for meaning and direction. I kept hearing His voice telling me to develop nonprofit Christian Sober Living homes. That has become our mission. That is our faith put into action.

You can always ask questions of God. You can show weakness or display sadness and confusion. But bitterness is a terrible response, akin to saying you don't trust God. Bitterness is a poison that can tear your life apart.

We don't grow muscles without resistance. And we don't grow faith by sitting around saying, "I want more faith." Faith needs to be built. Faith needs to be tested. Faith needs to be reinforced and strengthened. Faith needs a challenge, which is why God allows circumstances to test and build our faith.

God grows our faith the hard way, through trials and tribulations that test us to our core. How we react to each is how we build our faith muscle. Faith is knowing that God is working out His perfect plan in our lives. Sometimes we must wait, endure, and suffer. But faith makes all things possible.

God wants us to have a strong and vigorous faith, not a wafer-thin brand of faith that collapses like a tent in a windstorm. Faith makes things possible. It doesn't always make them easier. No matter what setbacks you face, God will never stop loving you. Know by faith that He has a plan for you that is good, and He cares about every detail of your life. God is always in control, and He is never surprised. No matter how much pain you experience, God is protecting you.

Faith is believing in His promises even when it seems like He isn't listening. Living by faith means living with supreme confidence that God will always honor His word and keep His promises. And being in communication with Him daily is the most effective way to see that He is doing just that. We may not always understand His methods, but they include a bigger picture and incorporate a greater understanding of everything unfolding in His plan that we can't always see.

"If you were to take the dictionary out of my office and look up the word 'impossible', you wouldn't find it. It isn't in there because I cut it out. I decided if it's not in God's dictionary, it's not going to be in mine." — Rick Warren

---

God is always testing our character, trying to shape us and strengthen us to handle the next rough spot with more grace and wisdom, without worry and fear. He wants us to show and grow our faith as we obey Him, whether we understand His reasons or not.

One important thing to remember is that no matter where God leads you, nowhere on earth is your forever home. We have an eternal home with Him, and that is what He is preparing us for. That is the ultimate destination we are moving toward.

The Source of Our Faith

Jesus reminds us that animals and plants don't worry. Birds don't say, "I'd better build a bigger nest for retirement." Only human beings fail to trust what God will provide for us. (See Matthew 6:25–34.) He meets even our smallest need when we call on Him, but He has already provided for our greatest need: salvation.

Jesus died on the cross so our sins would be forgiven and we would no longer have to live with guilt. He didn't just die for the sins we've already committed. He also died for the ones we haven't committed yet. That's a steal of a deal, in my opinion. And it's all covered under one cross.

And the resurrection that followed His crucifixion proves that Jesus is exactly who He claimed to be. He repeatedly said He was the Son of God who came to die for our sins so that we could have life, and life to the full (John 10:10). The resurrection proves that there is life after death. Jesus paid the price we could never pay so eternity in heaven with God would be secure for everyone who believes.

One of the ways you know that Jesus is at the center of your life is when you find yourself worrying less. Any time you start worrying, it should be a red flag, a warning sign that says, "I've allowed someone or something to become the center of my life instead of God." If Jesus is at the center, your life will be eternally blessed. The choice is yours: Are you going to live a life that is self-centered or God-centered?

Noah had tremendous faith. He heeded God's warning that the world was about to be destroyed. He believed and acted on what he had not yet seen. Remember, the definition of faith is being certain of something we don't see and doing what is right even when it seems absurd.

You'll find another great example in the story of Gideon in Judges 7. Gideon took 300 Israelites to battle 135,000 enemy soldiers. Their odds of success were 450–1. God instructed the soldiers to come armed with torches, trumpets, and clay pots. It's a command that I'm sure Gideon found ludicrous. But he went ahead and did what he was instructed to do because he trusted God.

Gideon, Job, Noah, and many others in the Bible were persistent in their faith, and God rewarded them for it. Walking in faith means you don't give up even when you're tired or can't see where the road is headed. It means pressing on even when you feel hopeless. God will give you strength to persevere. You can't live by faith without some degree of risk. But God sees the big picture with perfect clarity, and you can always trust what He's asking you to do.

If we put our trust in God, we can accomplish more than we've ever dreamed possible. God is always looking for the faithful people He can use to spread His Word and His love in a world full of desperation and confusion. God also knows that too many people pay lip service to the power of faith. They can talk the talk and say all the right things when necessary, but they don't walk with faith because they don't fully trust Him when the road gets rough. Faith means continuing to persist without knowing how long you'll need to hang on. And sometimes that's very difficult. So how do you continue in faith when you are suffering? How do you develop endurance? How do you handle prolonged pain?

You do what Moses did: you get close to God and stay connected so you can hear from Him. From this point on, march forward with God, without fear and without hesitancy. The next time you are overcome with fear, reject it all and see where it takes you. When you face the opposition and choose worship over worry, powerful things occur.

When you face the opposition and choose worship over worry, powerful things occur.

When I was a kid, I didn't worry about anything I needed in my life. Instead, I just went to my dad or mom and told them what I needed. I was never once concerned about how they were going to meet our needs because they took on that responsibility every time without fail. God wants you to be the same way with Him.

Pride is the trap that so often keeps Christians from being able to ask for and to give forgiveness. When we think we've got it all together, we don't make the effort to become more spiritually mature and to have the humility necessary to see that everyone makes mistakes, and that we all are in need of forgiveness more than we'd like to admit.

Pride not only keeps you from being open to the possibility that God might want to say something to you; it also ruins relationships by producing misunderstanding. It says, "I know it all; I don't need to listen." Pride provokes arguments because it says, "Look at how good I am."

I confess that I have fallen short of God's perfect standards. I have often failed many times to live with humility, and I know I need to be quicker confessing my sins to Christ, which requires humility and transparency.

God repeatedly tells us that if we humble ourselves before the Lord that He will bless us and give us peace. But pride keeps us from seeking God. It is important that we accept our human limitations and imperfections. The greatest barrier to change in any area of our lives is pride, because it keeps us from being honest about the areas where we need to change.

"Jesus said, 'If you hold to my teaching, you are really my disciples. Then you will know the truth, and the truth will set you free.'" — John 8:31–32

The Bible says there's nothing perfect on earth except God's Word. Everything on this planet is broken because of sin, so we need to humbly assess our current situation and put aside our pride. Why is it so important to see ourselves accurately? Because we can manage only what we can measure.

God is quick to give us grace when we mess up. Even when you do ridiculously bad things, God won't stop loving you. It truly is amazing grace.

You may have gone to God multiple times for forgiveness even on the same issue. Maybe you're not sure you deserve His love and grace—you can settle that now: You don't deserve it—and maybe you're convinced God has grown tired of your constant efforts at change. I can assure you He hasn't.

God never tires of a conversation with you. He's never too busy. No matter how many times you go to Him for forgiveness, He'll always be waiting with open arms.

"When Jesus stretched out his hands on the cross and said, 'Father, forgive them, for they do not know what they are doing,' nobody earned it or asked for it. Jesus took the initiative and offered forgiveness." — Rick Warren

---

Does this mean you can go about your life and not worry about what you do because you're forgiven? Of course not. Forgiveness does not free you from the consequences that come from poor decisions. You can be forgiven and still have regrets. You can be forgiven and still face pain. You can be forgiven and still have a broken relationship.

I believe forgiveness starts in the mirror. We need to know how to forgive ourselves in areas where we have behaved poorly or left a mess in our wake. Maybe you've done some horrible things in your life. Maybe you feel too ashamed to ask for God's forgiveness. Or maybe you feel unworthy of His grace. My pastor, Jamie Rasmussen, has said, "God isn't mad at us. He's mad *about* us!" And the first great freedom of the Christian life is a clear conscience. It's what occurs when God takes a giant eraser and forgives all your sins and wipes away all your guilt.

We all make mistakes we regret, and we need to seek forgiveness. Whenever you stumble or fall, confess your sin quickly and ask for God's help in the future. But don't keep beating yourself up over forgiven sin. Remember: in His wondrous grace, God is slow to chide and swift to bless.

Heading in the Right Direction

Sometimes God puts adversity in our path to keep us humble, as He did with the apostle Paul. When Paul talked about the "thorn in my flesh," he said, "Three times I pleaded with the Lord to take it away from me" (2 Corinthians 12:8). He struggled just as we struggle with being human and having human faults. He didn't want to keep repeating mistakes, and he asked God to remove his vulnerability to temptation, but that's not how God works. As we discussed in the last chapter, temptation is all around us and part of being wrapped in flesh. What God offers us as a remedy is His strength to lean on so we don't give in to temptation and His grace and forgiveness for when we do fall.

Learning how to forgive ourselves and others the way God does is a great step in the right direction. But a key part of staying on the right path is combining your forgiveness with repentance. That's not just being sorry for what happened or (more often) for getting caught; it's truly regretting how your actions affected your relationships with family, friends, coworkers, neighbors, and your relationship with God. It means truly wanting to change the behavior, not just wanting to get out of the consequences of the behavior.

The only way to have true repentance—which is the only thing that leads to taking steps in the right direction—is to be honest about your weaknesses and recognize your strengths as gifts from God. You do this by giving yourself checkups. Try this: Wake up every day and ask God, "What do I need to work on today?" This takes humility because it means you have to admit every day that you don't have it all together, but it's a habit that will lead to happiness.

Happiness and humility go together because they prompt you to ask important questions such as, How can I be a better spouse? How can I be a better friend? How can I be a better boss? How can I better follow Jesus?

Pope Francis correctly noted that "man is too preoccupied, too self-centered, and too selfish." And when you're preoccupied, you're not asking the right questions. You're missing out because you've stopped growing. And God made you to grow.

If you have sinned, don't hide in the corner, don't run from God. Remember that forgiveness is yours because God wants to be in relationship with you. He wants to have the air cleared so you can have open, honest communication. That means forgiving yourself, forgiving others, and humbly going to Him for forgiveness every time something creates distance or discord. We will never run out of chances to be forgiven, so we should be willing to give the same to those who need it from us.

Hope When It Looks Hopeless

It is also important to remember that growing our faith isn't automatic. God is working to draw you closer to Him, but you must also take steps to strengthen your faith. Here are some ways to do that:

1. *Make daily appointments with God.* Your faith will grow when you set aside time to talk to Him and read His words. The Bible will fully equip you for everything God wants you to do, and prayer is a simple conversation with God. He wants to hear anything you have to say, but make it a habit to ask for His forgiveness for your sins, help with your problems, and direction for your decisions.

2. *Learn all you can by reading Christian books.* Do yourself a favor and keep feeding your soul with what other believers have to say.

3. *Be faithful to a small group of believers.* You need a place to share burdens and celebrate your victories. You need a committed group of people who are praying for you. You also need to do these same things for others. We are better together because we help one another strengthen our faith.

Faith unlocks the promise of God and gives you the power to hold on in tough times. But it is important to understand that just because you have faith, God won't necessarily take you out of difficult circumstances. He may leave you in them to grow your faith.

Corrie ten Boom was a young Dutch Christian. She helped many Jews escape the Holocaust during World War II; for that reason, she was sent to a Nazi concentration camp. She said the people in those camps who refused to give up were the ones with the deepest faith. Why? Because faith gives you the power to hold on in tough times.

Faithful people remain hopeful even when things seem hopeless. In fact, God uses difficult circumstances to test your faith. He wants you to stay determined, persistent, and obedient, regardless of how confusing things may seem.

Consider the testimony of Noah that we touched on earlier. God warned him about things to come, and in obedience, Noah built the ark even though he had never seen rain. Sometimes we gloss over the fact that building the ark wasn't a quick weekend project; it took more than fifty years to complete! The ark was as tall as a four-story building, as long as one and a half football fields, and as wide as a tennis court is long.

In faith, Noah never gave up. Imagine how Noah's neighbors must have mocked and ridiculed him. But he didn't give up—he trusted God. Experiencing the first rain, the flood, and forty days on the ark would have also required faith. After the flood, Noah and his family had to start over with nothing but dependence on God and what He provided for them. That's resilient faith!

No matter how bad things may seem right now, don't give up. It's always too soon to quit! God is testing your faithfulness. Rivers never go in reverse . . . so try to love like a river. Forget your past and focus on your future.

SCRIPTURE FOR FAITH

"I have fought the good fight, I have finished the race, I have kept the faith." (2 Timothy 4:7)

———

"Without faith it is impossible to please God." (Hebrews 11:6)

———

"In every situation, by prayer and petition, with thanksgiving, present your requests to God. And the peace of God, which transcends all understanding, will guard your hearts and your minds in Christ Jesus." (Philippians 4:6–7)

———

"Be still before the LORD and wait patiently for him." (Psalm 37:7)

———

"Pride brings a person low, but the lowly in spirit gain honor." (Proverbs 29:23)

———

"For those who exalt themselves will be humbled, and those who humble themselves will be exalted." (Matthew 23:12)

CHAPTER 14

WHY I CAN BE INFLUENCED BY THE WORLD

"In the broken world, no matter who
is president, Jesus is King."

*T*hroughout the Bible, we know that it says that the world is broken. Jesus says numerous times that there's no peace in this world, and we are not to love this world.

Mike Krzyzewski, the Hall of Fame basketball coach who built a dynasty at Duke, always believed that his teams represented something bigger than themselves. When he coached Team USA to Olympic gold medals in 2008, 2012, and 2016, he stressed that the team represented America and that they had standards, not rules. He created a culture of excellence built on respect and honesty. Those are qualities we need in today's world.

One man who embodied those qualities was Gamboa, a Las Vegas cab driver who stumbled on a fortune in 2014. It was near Christmas, and a high-stakes poker player had accidentally left $300,000 in the back seat of Gamboa's taxi. The money was stashed inside a shopping bag in six separate stacks of $100 bills. Gamboa didn't even notice the prize left behind until he pulled up at the Bellagio Hotel for his next fare. That's when a bellman needed to make room for his passengers and placed the shopping bag next to Gamboa, on the front seat of the cab. Gamboa peeked inside. And in the face of great temptation, he did the unthinkable: He turned in the money to his supervisors, and through the Las Vegas police, they were able to find the rightful owner, who gave Gamboa a $10,000 reward.

Stories like Gamboa's remind us that there is still goodness and hope in the world. But why do examples of honesty and human compassion seem so rare in today's world?

I don't believe it is because they are in short supply. I think it is because we tend to focus more on the negative. We are conditioned to concentrate on our own needs first, so anyone not doing that seems like an anomaly.

My two favorite heroes growing up were Jackie Robinson of the Brooklyn Dodgers and Goose Tatum with the Harlem Globetrotters. Both happened to be Black. Since I was a young boy, and still in my adult years, I have never considered the color of the skin on a man or woman.

However, in the world, I know there has been tremendous discrimination against Black people, which has always bothered me. The world still experiences racism, which is prejudice against people based on their race or ethnicity.

In 1976, when I owned the Phoenix Racquets in World Team Tennis, the number-one tennis player in the world, Chris Evert, played on my team. I knew that Jesse Owens, who was in his seventies at the time, was living in Phoenix. I contacted Jesse to introduce myself and came up with an idea where Chris would put on a tennis clinic in the inner city primarily for Black children.

Together, Chrissie and Jesse conducted a tennis clinic for three hundred African American boys and girls at the Salvation Army. Chris had never done something like that before, and she was fabulous. She was trying to teach proper groundstroke techniques, and the kids kept hitting the tennis ball like it was a baseball. But Chris has tremendous patience, and the event was a smashing success.

My goal, knowing how much prejudice there is in the world that results in hatred, was to set an example where the top tennis player in the world and one of the greatest track stars ever, Jesse Owens, could come together without being concerned about the color of anyone's skin and put on a tennis clinic. It was a great moment, watching these children with smiles on their faces hitting tennis balls with Chris Evert.

Owens had set a world record in the running broad jump (now called the long jump) that stood for twenty-five years and had won four gold medals at the 1936 Berlin Olympic Games, in front of Adolf Hitler. Owens equaled the world record for the 100-yard dash (9.4 sec.) and broke the world records for the 220-yard dash (20.3 sec.), the 220-yard low hurdles (22.6 sec.), and the long jump (8.13 meters [26.67 feet]).

One popular account that arose from his victories was that of the "snub," the notion that Hitler refused to shake hands with Owens because he was African American.

Of course, the challenges we faced then and still face today go far beyond ethnic strife. In so many ways life on earth has always been a dicey proposition. Our world is broken, and it seems to be coming apart more and more by the day. We are jaded, angry, and divided by our differences. We are polarized by politics, besieged by crime, and beset with racial tensions. We have lost much of our civility, if not our humanity.

When we are hungry for success, we get caught in the trap of defining success by the terms the world sets forth for us, and that puts us in a rat race to get more, go bigger, and step on anyone who is in our way of getting where we think we need to be. Matthew 16:26 reminds us, "What good will it be for someone to gain the whole world, yet forfeit their soul?"

We forget that success is living an honorable and decent life, serving others, and making the world a better place—being better spouses, better friends, better parents, better role models, better business leaders, and better humans. We forget that when we serve others and turn our focus to the collective, away from selfish, vain, and narcissistic attitudes, we ultimately end up ensuring our own success.

It's so easy to get caught up in distractions, and when we love the world's value system, there's not much room to love people. Instead, we love materialism. We love pleasure. We love popularity and prestige. We love passion, possessions, and position.

The world is telling us that we need to get happier, more successful, more important, more valuable, and more secure. We have become unhinged in our pursuit of money, fame, and power. We chase clout. We worship celebrities and don't acknowledge the real heroes standing right in front of us.

The United States was once the subject of global envy—the nation with the highest standard of living on the planet—yet

America couldn't even crack the Top 20 list of the 2024 World Happiness Report, which uses global survey data to report how people evaluate their own lives in more than 150 countries. Finland was rated as the happiest nation, followed by Denmark, Iceland, Sweden, Israel, Netherlands, Norway, Luxembourg, Switzerland, and Australia. The United States landed at twenty-third.[3]

So, what are we missing when we seem to have everything we could possibly want or need? Why are many of us wandering in the world, seemingly lost and dissatisfied?

The Problem We Face

Addictions to sex, money, intoxicants, and distractions consume us as a society, and rather than offering ways to heal the inherent needs that drive these addictions, many actually encourage these unhealthy ways of seeking satisfaction.

"Let's face it: We live in a world where there is a spiritual buffet. It is called, 'Believe in Anything You Want That Feels Good.' And that might mean going along with whatever the crowd is doing."

— Jamie Rasmussen, senior pastor,

Scottsdale Bible Church

We are confronted with problems in our society, in ourselves as individuals, and in the faith that could restore us. It's not enough for me to point out all the societal ills we face; I am not doing anyone any favors if I only complain about a problem, so I want to point you to some answers as well. But first let's look at what needs to change. Then we'll talk about how to change it.

Societal Struggles

Our society is struggling, and we are looking to lots of different places for answers and often coming up empty. We are obsessed with the wrong types of entertainment, we don't know how to connect with each other, and we have lost our ability to be compassionate.

Technology is a big part of our challenge. We are not only addicted to the immediate gratification provided by smartphones, tablets, and laptops but are awed by the power of human invention and advancements in science, amazed at how technology can transform our lives as well. The World Wide Web was created at the end of the twentieth century, and within twenty-five years, it has changed the course of human behavior. Now we are on the doorstep of another technological revolution—the dangerous frontier of artificial intelligence (AI)—and I believe, in the process, we are in danger of being less awed by God, the one true Creator.

Technology has also made the world smaller. It has made the world louder. It has filled the world with social media platforms and paved the way for internet trolls. It has completely changed the rules of human engagement, and anonymity is a convenient shield on social media, affording users a stunning lack of accountability. That breeds a world without manners—a world where decency and empathy are diminished and violence is escalating. There is much hatred in the world, and we are seeing a lot of it start to divide our United States.

Another challenge we face as a society is that the desire for money and possessions is running rampant and pulling us farther and farther away from God. In America, success is usually defined by money, power, and fame. We have not learned that being financially successful is not the ultimate victory in life, and we often fall into the wealth trap.

"We are a divided country, and Satan is laughing at us. Because that is exactly what he wants. Dysfunction, mistrust, and hatred help his kingdom flourish. We have to realize we are not fighting against other people. We are fighting against Satan and his kingdom of spiritual darkness." — Tony Dungy, former NFL head coach and Super Bowl champion

---

The Problem as Individuals

As humans, we instinctively focus on serving ourselves—our needs, our wants, our impulses—and that's built in for self-preservation; but we have pushed that to the point where we no longer believe in the power of the communal good and the philosophy of going far together. We tend to believe we can go farther and faster alone.

We also get bogged down in our own suffering. Sometimes it's hard to understand why we have to suffer. It doesn't seem fair. We wonder, *Why I am going through this when other people aren't?* Maybe you've thought, *Why am I single when all my friends are married?* Or, *Why can't we have children when my friend has five?* Or, *Why do I have this horrible illness while all of my friends are healthy?*

When we are in the midst of suffering, it is hard to remember that good things happen to bad people, and bad things happen to good people. (See Matthew 5:45.) We live in a fallen and broken world, so we will inevitably have problems.

We are going to face times of trial and testing. It's guaranteed ever since sin entered the world. Everything on this planet is in a state of brokenness on some level—the weather, the economy, our bodies, and even our best plans. Nothing works perfectly because sin has impacted everything on earth. The Bible is very clear that earth is not heaven. It is an imperfect place that is full of sin because God has given us freedom of choice, and many people choose poorly.

"Our souls are not hungry for fame, comfort, wealth, or power ... [but] for meaning, for the sense that we have figured out how to live so that our lives matter, so that the world will be at least a little better for our having passed through it." — Rabbi Harold Kushner

---

No one is insulated from pain or gets to sail through life problem-free. The way of the world essentially guarantees there will be pressure and stress in our lives, and so many of us don't know where to turn for help.

The Problem in Faith

We are in a world that doesn't value God, and our own tendency to pursue our own way over obedience to His instruction leads us to make selfish, short-term decisions that aren't centered on God's teachings or a heaven-bound mindset.

Some people look for power in all the wrong places. Some look in self-help books, therapy, or the latest personal care trends. Some look in a promotion or pay raise. Most people in the modern secular world have difficulty making sense of life. The more disconnected from God our lives become, the more meaningless life becomes. When religion begins to lose its foundational roots, people indulge their worst tendencies. They seek to receive their heavenly rewards on earth in the form of material possessions and short-term gratification.

Recent studies have provided a stark picture of the lack of religious foundation sweeping through our country. Many people are moving away from biblical principles, even those who claim to follow Jesus. These are some of the startling findings I read in one of Rick Warren's newsletters:

- a "biblical" worldview is held by less than 6 percent of Americans;
- almost 70 percent of self-proclaimed born-again Christians don't believe Jesus is the only way to God; and
- a record-low 20 percent of the US population views the Bible as God's "actual Word."[4]

If you attempt to live a godly life, your very presence can be an irritant to some. The example you are trying to set is a rebuke to the person who isn't living according to God's Word. But those people are not irritated by you; they are irritated by what you stand for, what you believe, and who you are following. In today's world, it's not considered cool to be a committed Christian, which is a shame, because I believe if we all lived like Christians, we could turn this thing around. And wouldn't it be great if all the people who claim to be Christians started acting like it?

Some people are surprised to find that it isn't easy being a Christian. Once we put our faith in Christ, we immediately find that we have an adversary (the devil) who wants to bring us down. The world wants to pull our kids away from God's Word and the truth it shares. Young people need to know what God's Word says about the hot topics in the world right now so they can choose better.

"Do not conform to the pattern of this world, but be transformed by the renewing of your mind." — Romans 12:2

Remember, in this world God is more interested in us being *faithful* than being *successful*. You can reach the highest pinnacle in business and in life, but if you don't have the Lord, it's not going to fulfill you. God wants us to prosper. However, He won't bless us if we're motivated by greed, guilt, selfishness, fear, or pride. God is more interested in what you're becoming than in what's happening to you. He often allows trials, troubles, tribulations, and problems to teach you diligence, determination, and character. The problem you're going through right now is a test of your faithfulness. Will you continue to serve God when the going gets tough?

The longer I live and the more I study, the more I'm convinced that God's Word is the only thing that will change our families, our communities, our culture, and our broken world. We live in a very confusing time and there is much I don't understand; that's why I turn to two words: *Trust God!* As we wait for God to reveal all the details, the prophetic Scriptures can strengthen us, encourage us, and give us certain hope.

We will find the true happiness we seek only in a relationship with God. The happy life is the life with God, so don't settle for some cheap imitation this world offers.

I could take you to some of the poorest places in the world and show you two people living right next door to each other.

One is miserable and one is happy. Happiness has nothing to do with your circumstances and everything to do with your attitude. If you're not happy with what you have right now, I can guarantee that you're not going to be happy with more, because no matter what you have, you're always going to want a little bit more.

To have a happy heart, you have to practice service and generosity every day. Those two things will bring more happiness than anything else, and they define what it means to follow Jesus. If you're not serving, if you're not giving, then you're not following Jesus. It's very simple.

This world is not all there is, and that's a good thing, because sometimes things get pretty bad. As believers, one of the reasons we have hope is because, no matter how bad it seems on earth, we know it's only temporary. After death, we get to spend eternity with God. In heaven, there will be no more sorrow, no more sadness, no more sickness, and no more suffering (Revelation 21:4).

The Big Three principles we are given in the Bible are faith, hope, and love (1 Corinthians 13:13). The Bible is full of hope and promise for our world, our individual lives, and our eternal lives. But if we are looking only at our earthly life and not spending enough time with the Lord and studying His Word, we have a diminished view of God and an exalted view of this world. It should be the other way around.

"May the God of hope fill you with all joy and peace as you trust in him, so that you may overflow with hope by the power of the Holy Spirit." — Romans 15:13

One day Jesus Christ will govern the world and His knowledge will touch every life. However, the only way to experience lasting change in this world is by believing in Jesus as your Savior. He provides the power you need to become who God created you to be.

Our Hope in Society

Because the flesh is weak, we all face the temptation to seek the pleasures of the world rather than putting God first. We will not find the answer in any of those places because the answer is not a place, a program, or a pill. The answer is a person: Jesus Christ.

And the good news is we don't have to settle; we don't have to go through life just existing. We were not created to just coast along. God made each of us for a mission and a purpose. When we commit our lives to understanding God's will, we can live in obedience to Him. And maybe the most important mission we have is the Great Commission to go out into the world and share God's love and the hope that is found in Him and in salvation (Matthew 28:19).

Even though I've mentioned the problems technology presents for us as a society, I do believe God can give us a vision for how technology can be used to spread the gospel. Technology has unleashed the worst of us, but it can also harness and empower our best attributes.

Consider the story of Kevin Ford, a Burger King employee at Harry Reid International Airport in Las Vegas. Ford, fifty-four years old, had spent half his life working for the fast-food giant. He'd never missed a shift and never called in sick. Like sunrise, he showed up every day, and when his twenty-seventh anniversary arrived, Burger King rewarded him with a backpack filled with a movie ticket, a Starbucks cup, and an assortment of candy. Video of the event went viral and people were outraged at the paltry gift. A GoFundMe page was set up, and at last count, donations exceeded $450,000.[5]

That uplifting story is a reminder of how good we can be when we rally around each other and how technology can facilitate and expedite the process. In a similar vein, it's my heart's desire to spread the gospel to as many people as possible and as quickly as possible.

I have also partnered with my friend Jerry Colangelo, former majority owner of the Phoenix Suns and Arizona Diamondbacks, in using technology to combat the negativity around us. We produced faith-based broadcasts featuring influential people who had suffered unimaginable losses and told their stories of how faith got them through. We had gifted musicians perform inspiring songs to help deliver messages of hope.

I believe it is important for us as a society to spread these messages of hope and direct people to where it is found so those who are in seasons of loss and pain will know they do not have to endure it alone.

Our Hope as Individuals

We don't understand everything we face in the world we live in today because we are human. We can't grasp all of God's plans and methods, but we can trust His sovereignty. In addition to His holiness, His purity, and His power, He is love and goodness. He cares about the details of our lives.

God's Holy Spirit wants to work in our lives. The question is, Do we want Him to work? The Bible says, "Do not quench the Spirit" (1 Thessalonians 5:19). Sometimes God's Holy Spirit will nudge us to do a certain thing or go to a certain place, and we'll say no. That is quenching the Spirit. To have the spiritual awakening we crave, we need the Holy Spirit at work in our lives, empowering us, filling us so we can deal with this broken world we live in.

We all are *blessed to be a blessing*. That's a hopeful, encouraging truth to remember. In a world that urges us to just look out for ourselves, we must find ways to be radically generous to the people God has placed in our lives. When we do that, we get regular reminders of how blessed we are because we see what we are capable of doing for others.

Our Hope in Faith

No matter how difficult the adversity and challenges we face, God will help us. We should not fear, for He is with is. He will give us the strength we need when we trust Him and do what He says. The safest place for us to be is right in the middle of His will. The Savior who was with us in the beginning is the same God who will be with us until the end. He is our Alpha and Omega (Revelation 1:8). Everything that happens to us from birth to death is in His hands. Don't let the confusion of the world distress you. We can live in joyful confidence because of Christ.

Jesus promises that we will have problems in this world, which is why fellowship with other believers is important. Fellowship is more than socializing. We may talk about all kinds of things at church, but our primary reason is to talk about the things of God.

It is a powerful testimony to the world when a Christian can praise God despite their problems and hardships. Believers face the same hardships that nonbelievers face. But when they see us praising God despite adverse circumstances, when they see us honoring the Lord, that is a powerful testimony. Our worship can be a witness even when our problems grow bigger and bigger; by trusting God we receive a peace that the world doesn't understand and that the world cannot match—it can't even come close!

That's right: God's peace is not something you work for or beg for. It's a gift you receive by faith. Turn to God in prayer and tell Him what's on your mind. Focus on His goodness, and His perfect peace will fill your heart and mind, which will help you with the problems you face.

Theologian Charles Spurgeon battled depression throughout his life and yet he had a great ministry. He said even when he was greatly discouraged, he still had joy because he trusted God.

You might be in the middle of a season filled with problems and trials. Understanding that our trials develop us so we can help others allows us to have hope for a better outcome and for weathering the storms. God will never waste a hurt. God will work *in* your life so He can work *through* your life to impact others. And the world closely watches how Christians handle adversity.

One of the greatest questions we can ask ourselves is, *Does my life change other people's lives for the better?* We all win when we put others first. God also wired the universe in such a way that the more you give yourself away, the more God gives to you and the more blessed and the happier you are.

"'For I know the plans I have for you,' declares the LORD, 'plans to prosper you and not to harm you, plans to give you hope and a future.'" — Jeremiah 29:11

The Promise of Restoration

When a person lifts weights, they strain, stretch, and stress their muscles. That's how they grow stronger. Hope and faith are like a muscle, and the only way to build them is to put them to the test.

Faith isn't the absence of worry; it's moving forward with what God wants, even in the face of doubt and uncertainty.

In this world it often seems like we are too busy to spend time with God, which is the only way to develop that faith muscle. Billy Sunday became one of the great evangelists of his generation. When he was a new believer, an older Christian gave him this advice: take fifteen minutes each day to let God talk to you, allow fifteen minutes to talk to Him, then spend fifteen minutes telling others about the Savior. He told Billy that if he did these three things, no one would ever consider that he was not a true Christian.

If you have a relationship with God and are walking closely with Him, then you will see this world for what it is. You will recognize the philosophies, concepts, and ideologies that contradict what the Bible teaches. When you are walking closely with God, you also will see the emptiness and the futility of the things that people chase after.

Walking in this world is going to come with difficulties and disappointments, problems and pain, but we have the promise of hope and restoration that comes from God's Word. That is a firm foundation where we can set our feet as we go forward.

"Our citizenship is in heaven." — Philippians 3:20

Maybe you've seen the popular bumper sticker, "He who dies with the most toys wins!" Millions of people act like that bumper sticker is true, but it couldn't be more misleading. A more accurate saying is, "He who dies with the most toys still dies, and never takes his toys with him."

If we devote our lives to acquiring things, we don't win at the end. We lose. We move into eternity, but our toys stay behind, filling the saddest of human junkyards. And too many people, including me, have spent too much time searching for life in the wrong places: chasing pleasures, accumulations, possessions, power, and wealth.

We need to heed the words of Psalm 49:16–17: "Don't be dismayed when the wicked grow rich and their homes become ever more splendid. For when they die, they take nothing with them. Their wealth will not follow them into the grave" (NLT).

Too often, personal success in America is celebrated for the wrong reasons, contrary to what God requires. In Matthew 6:19–20, Jesus said, "Don't store up treasures here on earth, where moths eat them and rust destroys them, and where thieves break in and steal. Store your treasures in heaven, where moths and rust cannot destroy, and thieves do not break in and steal" (NLT).

Jesus also said that many who are first now will be last then, and some who are last now will be first then (Matthew 20:16). That was and is a warning to those who inflate their own goodness, who believe attending church and donating old clothes to charity is enough to prove your worth before God.

As we wrap up this chapter, let's remember that God can't be evil. God doesn't just *do* good things, God *is* good. Everything that is good in this world comes from Him. God is good all the time, and that means that His plans for your life are good. You don't have to wonder or worry about your future, because God has that covered. Your hope for tomorrow is secure. The only reason there is any good in the world is because God, our Creator, is a good God. If there is no God, then there is no right and wrong, no good and bad.

At the same time, we all know that evil exists and too often influences our thoughts, words, and actions (or lack of actions).

Why? Because God gave us free choice. God doesn't force us to do good, so we sometimes choose the opposite.

"And this world is fading away, along with everything that people crave. But anyone who does what pleases God will live forever." — 1 John 2:17 NLT

Everyone in the world is born with a sinful nature. Make no mistake about it: We are sinners to the core. We don't have to teach our children how to sin. It comes quite naturally to them, just as it comes naturally to us. We aren't sinners because of the sin; we sin because we are sinners.

Yet God shows us what we can become by His grace. It is by believing in and living out this hope of becoming more and more of who God designed and destined us to be that we can become less and less influenced by this broken world—which, thanks be to God, is only our temporary dwelling place and not the ultimate home for those who place our faith in Jesus Christ.

CHAPTER 15

WHY I CARE ABOUT
THE POOR

"The true measure of our character
is how we treat the poor."

I like to put a smile on the faces of homeless people any chance I can get. One of the outlets that the Lord has blessed me with to help those in need is through the wonderful mission of the Society of St. Vincent de Paul. Every year on January 17 in honor of Muhammad Ali's birthday at my local St. Vincent de Paul, I organize a steak dinner for approximately five hundred homeless people. I contact several of the top chefs in Arizona, including Mark Tarbell, Chris Bianco, Marc Lupino, Vincent Guerithault, Christopher Gross, and celebrity chef Mark Candelaria. They love cooking for the event. It is always a choice steak, but we have to make sure it's cut up into little pieces, because many of the homeless are missing teeth. I am reminded of the scriptural command to "obey these instructions without taking sides or showing favoritism to anyone" (1 Timothy 5:21 NLT).

Howard Schultz, former CEO of Starbucks, was very poor growing up and lived in a housing project in Brooklyn. His strong work ethic helped him overcome extreme poverty, and today he is worth upward of $2.8 billion.[6]

We honored Howard at our Celebrity Fight Night charity event when he received the Muhammad Ali Humanitarian Award. We also honored another billionaire at our Celebrity Fight Night Charity Event who was also very poor growing up, John Paul DeJoria.

Growing up, John sold Christmas cards and newspapers as a child. He also collected pop bottles and sold them for two cents at the grocery store. Sadly, as an adult, John was broke and homeless and was sleeping in his car in his twenties. He overcame tough times. He was surviving on $2.50 a day. He said he had the resilience and determination required to overcome challenges. Today John, who founded Paul Mitchell, is worth $2.9 billion.[7]

Schultz and DeJoria are very generous by helping the poor. They understand the scars of being poor from when they were growing up, and now they are giving back to help those in need.

My brother Gary, when he was living, many times at Thanksgiving would bring one or two people to our family dinner who were needy and didn't have a place to go for Thanksgiving because they were poor.

Gary loved the poor. It's sad when you realize that in America, the land of opportunity, 12.4 percent of Americans now live in poverty according to new data from the 2022 US census.

Gary knew one of the better ways to help the poor and needy was to give them a hand up rather than a handout. Gary would give them moral support, and they knew that he really cared about them and was trying to improve their condition. I am thankful that I had an older brother like Gary who taught me by his example not to overlook the poor.

Can a person be poor and happy? Yes. I have been a volunteer at St. Vincent de Paul for many years, and I have met many homeless people whose lives are filled with joy, love, and fulfillment, beyond material possessions or financial stability because they had strong faith in God.

Steve Zabilski, Shannon Clancy, and Jerry Castro who work at St Vincent De Paul are shining examples for me since they live by the scripture "Don't show favoritism to the rich and look down upon the poor" (James 2:6).

As much as our words speak, so do our actions. As we invite people onto this journey of faith, our conduct can have as much influence on our witness as what we say. We are often so concerned about quoting the right scriptures and making the most convincing arguments that we forget that how we walk in faith makes a difference too.

I like to help the underdog. I like to reach out to those in crisis. Whenever I leave home, I make sure I have a stack of $5 McDonald's gift cards in my pocket, and I give them away to homeless people and those who might be rummaging through garbage cans.

I say hello while handing them a gift card. That gets their attention. Then I ask a question many haven't heard in years: "What's your name?"

You should see how their eyes light up when they hear that question. Too often, the homeless and the less fortunate are viewed as less than human and treated like they don't matter. Asking their name restores their dignity and shows them the respect many of them crave. I leave them all with this simple message: "God loves you and knows your potential."

My hope is that our brief interaction and a small gesture of kindness might spark the change necessary to find their former selves, to find their lost flame, to reclaim their lives. God is very clear on how we should treat the poor, and it is, in my opinion, one of the most important and effective ways we can share the gospel.

The Bible teaches us that servanthood is the defining quality of Christian leadership. It means helping people who can't help you back. It means helping people when no one is looking. It means helping the poor when they can be of no use to you. Anyone who helps the poor honors God and shows His love without ever having to say a word.

I believe many Christians are so hung up on morality and purity that they no longer care about the poor. They are ignoring God and one of the core tenets of Christian philosophy. There was a time when I didn't want to get my hands dirty either, but I was awakened to how that affected my witness.

My daughter Jennifer took a job at St. Vincent de Paul. Before I started hosting my annual dinner for the homeless there, she urged me to get involved as a volunteer, but I only paid lip service to her requests. I told her I was too busy. I felt pangs of shame and self-loathing immediately. Why was I so reluctant to serve the poor and the less fortunate, as God commands? What did that say about me?

When I finally volunteered in 2001, I encountered a homeless man who was extremely disheveled and in a state of very poor hygiene. He reached out to shake my hand. I recoiled. I failed.

"You don't want to shake my hand, do you?" he asked.

"Yes, I do," I lied.

"No, you don't," he said, walking away.

In that moment, God sent me clarity. I knew my heart was dirtier than that homeless man I just rejected and I needed to change. My witness was compromised.

St. Vincent de Paul has only one mission: to help the poor. Every time I visit, I feel like I am arriving at the University of Adversity. I meet people who are hurting tremendously, on the inside and the outside. They are in bad shape physically and spiritually. Many of them were knocked down by one obstacle too many. It breaks my heart, and it is far too common in today's world.

"If you want to be happy for an hour, eat a steak ... for a day, play a round of golf ... for a week, go on a cruise ... for a month, buy a car ... for a year, win the lottery. If you want to be happy for a lifetime, figure out how to add value to the lives of others." — Lou Holtz

---

I initiated a "Never Give Up" program at my local St. Vincent de Paul in Phoenix, a group that met every Monday morning at 7:00 a.m. for twelve consecutive years and only ended in 2020 due to the pandemic. The program grew to include a steady array of guest speakers. The list included businesspeople, doctors, attorneys, housewives, and celebrities. It warms my heart to say I've rarely had an athlete or entertainer turn down a chance to speak with the homeless. They all seem to rise to the occasion.

I took Muhammad Ali and his wife, Lonnie, many times to St. Vincent de Paul so the homeless could meet Ali. Muhammad loved the poor and nobody could put a smile on their face quicker than the Champ when he was spending time with them. Muhammad always wanted to help the poor and he was never too busy for them. I learned more about love from Muhammad than perhaps any person I've ever met. The champ could not spell the word *hate*, which is why the world loved him!

One time, I showed up to a Never Give Up meeting with the famous Italian singer and musician Andrea Bocelli. I picked up Bocelli at his hotel at 6:30 a.m., the morning after his concert in Arizona, which means he didn't get much sleep. It was also unseasonably cool for the desert, maybe 40° at best. It couldn't have been the best deal for his career and his billion-dollar voice. And yet Bocelli stood there, in front of the homeless, and sang "Ave Maria." I am not sure many of those in attendance even knew who Bocelli was or why he was singing one of the most famous Catholic prayers in Latin, but he sure sounded good.

Another time, former NBA superstar Dwyane Wade spoke at St. Vincent de Paul. He told the story of how his mother was once a homeless drug addict, living on the streets before finding Christ and turning her life around. Jolinda Wade founded her own church on the south side of Chicago, which was purchased by her famous son and dedicated to helping those in need. She is an inspiration to everyone she meets.

Baseball superstar legend Reggie Jackson spoke to about 500 homeless men and women at breakfast at St. Vincent de Paul and told them that he failed, striking out 2,597 times at the plate, which is a major league record. Reggie told them with his failing he did not quit, give up, and make excuses and shared that he made it to the Hall of Fame. Reggie then mentioned to the homeless that they can make it too by not giving up and quitting. Reggie received a standing ovation!

It can be challenging serving the poor. It will test your nerve. Many have learned not to trust a world that can be so horribly cruel. A homeless man once confronted me as I walked into St. Vincent de Paul.

"What are you doing here? Are you homeless? What do you know about being homeless? Are any of these celebrity speakers you bring here homeless?" he pressed.

"No, they are not homeless," I said. "But many of them have problems, just like you and me."

Another homeless man said to me, "I shouldn't even be in this room. I have held a gun to another man's head. I have broken into buildings and stolen things. I don't deserve to be here." I shook his hand. I told him none of us were worthy, and all of us required God's grace and forgiveness.

Do you know what else I've learned about the poor? They have a lot to teach those of us who are far more fortunate. After one of our meetings at St. Vincent de Paul, a homeless woman kept asking me to spell my name. I couldn't understand why. But she kept asking. She kept writing letters on a small piece of paper. And then she handed me a check for $10.

I refused her money, but she insisted. She said the gesture strengthened her faith. She said she needed to give. I was speechless. I had no idea what to do with the check. I didn't think I could ever cash it or put it in the bank, but I couldn't disrespect her incredible display of faith either.

A few hours a later, a ten-year-old boy walked into my office seeking donations. He was raising money for Muscular Dystrophy. I knew then that God had arranged both encounters so I could facilitate the gift. I gave the boy the $10 check. It felt perfect.

Every speaker I brought to St. Vincent de Paul delivered messages of hope and inspiration and resilience. And they all claim the experience changed their own lives more than their words helped the homeless. I know the feeling.

I have also learned that some of the most grateful people I know are those who possess very little. They've learned what little they have is a gift to be appreciated. While rich people have all the money, it seems like poor people have cornered the market on faith.

There are a lot of people out there who need assistance. And if you want to find true happiness in your life, then help the poor. You'll be amazed by the results.

When you learn the art of gratitude, life becomes much simpler. Gratitude makes us happy because it reminds us how fortunate we are.

There are many excuses to look the other way. There are many reasons to pass on the opportunity to share the gospel. But we are called to reach out to the less fortunate, whether they are facing physical hardships in daily life or are walking through life not knowing where they will spend eternity.

God tells us very clearly: to whom much is given, much is expected (Luke 12:48). He has given us grace. He has given us salvation. He has given us the promise of eternity with Him. And He expects us to offer the same gift to everyone we meet.

SCRIPTURE FOR HELPING THE POOR

"Speak up and judge fairly; defend the rights of the poor and needy." (Proverbs 31:9)

———

"Happy is the generous man, the one who feeds the poor." (Proverbs 22:9 TLB)

———

"When you help the poor you are lending to the Lord—and he pays wonderful interest on your loan!" (Proverbs 19:17 TLB)

———

"Better poor and humble than proud and rich." (Proverbs 16:19 TLB)

CHAPTER 16

WHY I WANT TO HELP PEOPLE TO BE SOBER

"Choosing to be sober will give you a better life."

*A*lice Cooper spends time with teenagers talking about the dangers of drugs and alcohol, which almost ruined Alice's life in the 1970s. He admits that cocaine and alcohol practically destroyed him until he got sober in 1983.

Alice has been my friend for about thirty years. We have played golf together—whenever he came up short on a putt he would say, "Hit the ball, Alice!"—attended Phoenix Suns games, and he has even participated with large boxing gloves in the Celebrity Fight Night charity event. Alice also spoke at our nonprofit Grace Sober Living home, encouraging men who are in recovery from drugs and alcohol.

Alice is very open about his faith in Jesus Christ. A lot of people say, "I came to Christ because of my love for Jesus." Alice says, "I came to Christ because of my fear of God. I totally understood that hell was not getting high with Jim Morrison. Hell was going to be the worst place ever. In fear, I came back to the Lord. I knew there had to be a point where I either accepted and started living that life, or if I died in this, I was in a lot of trouble. And that's what really motivated me.

"I'll tell you one thing, when Jesus opens your eyes, and you finally realize who you are, and who He is, it's a whole different world."[8]

Jerry Colangelo and I had Tony Dungy as one of our guest speakers on our faith-based broadcast. Tony was the first African American coach to win a Super Bowl in 2006 when his Indianapolis Colts beat the New England Patriots, 38–34.

Tony's son James had an ongoing problem with drugs and ended up taking his own life at age eighteen.

Coach Dungy says you may think you're in control of your life, but you're wrong if you're under the influence of alcohol or drugs because they can take over your mind and your memories. They make you do stuff when you don't want to and then make you forget that you've done anything. When you let drugs and alcohol into your life, you give up control and open yourself to terrible consequences.

Dying Too Young

I was born in 1944. Elvis was still singing, and Marilyn Monroe was on the silver screen. They each struggled with all the temptations that are afforded to those with fame, and they eventually lost the battle and died too young. Of course, decades have come and gone since then, but when I look at the young generation of today, it reminds me a lot of what was happening during my youth.

When we add social media to all these things our young people are dealing with, it's pouring gasoline on a fire. It amplifies everything. Self-harm among young people is up 334 percent.[9] The suicide rate in the United States has increased 30 percent since 2000.[10] This generation needs help. Instead, it's getting new kinds of drugs. It is important to recognize that any temptation can become an addiction, whether it's drugs, unhealthy food, the internet, sexual promiscuity, acquiring money and possessions, gossip, or any other substance, thought, or behavior that pulls you out of God's will. I just have a particular heart for helping people guard against drug abuse and addiction because of how it affected my family.

The latest epidemic has given our country a new "f-word"— fentanyl, a synthetic opioid that has spread to every corner of the illegal drug market, showing up in tainted heroin, cocaine, Adderall, and other drugs. Fentanyl is fifty times stronger than heroin and one hundred times more potent than morphine. Two milligrams of fentanyl is considered a lethal dosage, an amount so small that it could fit on the tip of a pencil.

It's a scary world, and the illegal production of fentanyl that crosses our border from Mexico remains the deadliest drug-related threat facing our nation. According to the Drug Enforcement Agency, a record number of Americans (107,622) died from drug poisoning or overdose in 2021. Over 66 percent of those deaths can be attributed to synthetic opioids like fentanyl.[11]

Our nation's current drug crisis has fueled lawlessness and homelessness in America. Our children have never been more vulnerable or at greater risk of lethal overdoses like the one that took the life of our son, Scott, at age forty-three. Both issues have hardened our collective perspective and increased our empathy for those afflicted, but I have also learned that drug and alcohol addiction is not a character flaw. It's a disease.

Unfortunately, I knew the dangers of drug addiction long before Scott's passing. I was working with NBA star Walter Davis on an insurance program for his family in 1987 when news broke of a cocaine scandal that would rock the NBA. They called it "Walter-gate." It was bad because Walter was such a great ambassador for the Suns. Everyone loved him and he always acted with class. He was Michael Jordan's favorite player. His one-year suspension from the NBA stunned everyone.

I went to Walter's house after the news broke, and we had an emotional visit that lasted two hours. I gave him a big hug and reminded him that we all make mistakes in life. I told him he had the opportunity to receive a fresh start by addressing the problems head-on, but he would have to deal with the consequences of his mistakes. Yet this would not change the fact that I would always support him.

"There's no better place to discover the healthiest possible response to loneliness than the Word of God." — Ruth Graham

---

We had weekly Bible study sessions, sometimes twice a week. I attended Alcoholics Anonymous meetings with Walter so he wouldn't have to go alone. I became one of his sponsors and often visited with him at the rehab center where he was treated.

We decided to hold fundraising dinners to raise money for charity to turn his struggles into something positive. We invited to our home in Phoenix his former teammates and friends from the NBA and the University of North Carolina, where Davis had been a collegiate star. The guest list included Michael Jordan, Charles

Barkley, James Worthy, Danny Ainge, Coach Dean Smith, John Lucas, Phil Ford, Mitch Kupchak, Sean Elliott, Charlie Scott, and Al Wood. It was a star-studded event, and we donated a sizable amount of money to drug treatment centers in Arizona.

Everyone loved Walter, who remained sober until he died of natural causes in November 2023.

Before the Grammys in 2012, I had hoped to inspire another star to find a different direction. Her name was Whitney Houston. I became briefly acquainted with Whitney at one of our Celebrity Fight Night events when we honored her agent and friend Clive Davis.

I knew she was attending Clive's party on the eve of the Grammys at the Beverly Hills Hotel—a coveted event for which I had somehow scored a ticket. I found out Whitney and I were staying at the same hotel. I had arranged to meet her at 4:00 p.m., following her rehearsal. I knew she was raised in a Christian setting, and I planned on praying with her and giving her a small wooden cross. I wanted the token gesture to be something she could hold on to that could give her strength.

I was preparing for our meeting when my phone rang and I learned of her passing. I ran into one of Whitney's associates in the lobby and told him I was supposed to sit down with her.

"Discouraged people don't need critics. They hurt enough already. They need encouragement." — Charles Swindoll

---

"Jimmy, let me take that cross," he said. "I'm going up to her room and I'm going to lay it on her."

After experiences like these, I have tried whenever possible to help those who have fallen, because I have seen firsthand how drugs and alcohol can tear apart souls and lives and families. And I saw how the pandemic in 2020 put our drug crisis over the top, creating additional stress on our daily lives, creating social isolation where depression and loneliness became significant issues.

The Void Left by Addiction

My son had a good bit of experience with rehabilitation centers, but he did not enjoy his experiences. He did not like how they were run and how they treated people. So many of them had making a profit as their main goal.

Scott was not a quitter. He was a successful businessman with a loving family. He tried twenty-seven times to defeat his addiction by going to detox. Could you imagine a heavyweight boxer getting up after twenty-seven knockdowns? They would be hailed for their courage and resiliency. But it's a different ball game when you're talking about drugs and alcohol and the stigmas that come with addiction.

Scott also attended three different thirty-day rehabilitation programs. Each time he was discharged, our family hoped and prayed that Scott would remain sober. We were hopeful because Scott was trying his best up until the relapse and accidental overdose that took his life far too soon.

Nothing tests your faith more than losing a child. I'll never forget the moment I learned about his death on December 12, 2019, and how my heart nearly exploded in my chest. As a family, we have grieved and endured, taking solace in knowing Scott is at home with the Lord, no longer suffering from his disease. We take great comfort knowing we will one day be reunited in the kingdom of heaven, and what a day that will be.

However, there is also a void in our lives that will never be truly whole or healed again. The grief is constant and powerful. It still brings me to my knees. Recently, I heard Andrea Bocelli's "Time to Say Goodbye" and broke down crying on the spot because we never had the chance to say goodbye.

I am not the same person I was before his death. I find myself praying more often. I spend more time reading the Bible. I spend more time hugging and appreciating my wife, Nancy. I also talk with Scott every day, and I thank him for helping me grow a deeper relationship with God. He was a gift from the Lord for Nancy and me.

"When you experience a loss, it's an opportunity to grow in character. You have to remember that, even in your pain, God is working for your good." — Rick Warren

---

I have learned that everyone grieves differently. But everyone grieves eventually. I have learned grief is the price to pay for losing a loved one. I have learned grief is painful but healthy. I have learned grief is a gift from God to help us through the toughest seasons in life. I have learned that faith is our shelter in the storm. Take the time to build your shelter—you will need it one day.

Scott had a deep love for God and people. Even while battling his own addiction, he felt compelled to help others. At his lowest points, he would often stuff his pocket with small wooden crosses, the same kind I had hoped to give Whitney Houston. He would hand them out to people in obvious need, people who were clearly broken and hurting. On many occasions, he told me of his desire to open his own nonprofit sober living home in Phoenix to combat the lack of good options in the Valley.

I promised him I would help him realize that dream, and I now dedicate my efforts to developing Grace Sober Living Homes, fulfilling Scott's vision for a Christian environment that would be run with honesty, integrity, and real empathy. We couldn't save Scott, but we are honoring his wishes of helping others with their recovery, and that's the best we can do—the best way to make something good from Scott's unfortunate passing, the best way to honor a special son I deeply loved who left this world far too soon.

Grace Sober Living won't stop drugs from coming into our country; however, we can save lives by helping addicts get sober.

As of this writing, Nancy and I, along with our daughters Laurie and Jennifer and our board, have started seven nonprofit sober living homes for men and one for women. We plan to develop more, but none of this would have been possible without Scott's influence to help other men and women who have the same disease.

As believers, we should commit to doing anything we can to change this course, call people to Christ, and pray for a mighty spiritual awakening to sweep our nation and beyond.

How to Face Your Temptations

As I've already said, the devil knows how to target our weak spots. He is relentless and has an army of demons who want to attack us at every turn. They work overtime to send temptations our way and are very good at catching us when our resolve is low or our guard is down.

So, how do you handle such an aggressive intruder? The Bible clearly says what to do with temptation: "Flee from all this" (1 Timothy 6:11). That means run. Don't walk. When you feel tempted to do something self-defeating, destructive, or dishonoring to God, you should move out of the situation rapidly. If you're watching something on television that stirs up feelings of lust, change the channel. If you struggle with alcohol, stay away from bars. And don't assume you are stronger than your temptations.

What do you fill your mind with? Have you noticed that the more you think about something, the more it takes hold of you? The Bible says if you want to overcome temptation, you need to resist the devil. How can you do that? By replacing tempting thoughts with biblical truth.

There are two steps you can take to prepare for battle:

1. Accept God's salvation as your helmet. What does a helmet do? It protects your mind, which is where the battle against temptation is fought.

Wouldn't it be great if we could reach a plateau in our lives as believers where we are somehow above all temptations and struggles? Well, that isn't going to happen. Temptation in our life never disappears. That is why we need the tools God has provided to protect ourselves from giving in to the temptations that are always there.

Ephesians 6:11–12 tells us, "Put on all of God's armor so that you will be able to stand firm against all strategies of the devil. For we are not fighting against flesh-and-blood enemies, but against evil rulers and authorities of the unseen world, against mighty powers in this dark world, and against evil spirits in the heavenly places" (NLT).

2. Pray. When you experience a moment of temptation or weakness, approach God through Christ with confidence to find mercy and grace in your time of need (Hebrews 4:16). Jesus will intercede for you because He has felt how you feel.

Jesus, during his earthly ministry, was always in sync, always in harmony, and always doing the things that pleased the Father. Yet the Holy Spirit led Jesus into the wilderness to face three temptations from the devil. Why? To show us what to do when temptation comes our way. To be a model for the rest of us.

During His temptation in the wilderness, Jesus could've said, "Satan, be gone!" And Satan would have left immediately. Jesus had that kind of authority and power over the devil. But He didn't do this. Instead, Jesus quoted Scripture.

He experienced the same pressures and temptations that we do. The reason He is without sin is because He didn't give in to them. Jesus suffered like us. He felt pain and disappointment. He became tired and lonely. He grieved, and He cried. Jesus became what we are so we can become what He is.

Jesus became what we are so we can become what He is.

When you think about things that aren't good for you, it's easy to fall into temptation. But when your mind focuses on something else, temptation loses its power. Focus instead on what is true, noble, right, pure, lovely, and honorable (Philippians 4:8). We can't give Satan power if we don't give him permission. In other words, when temptation calls, don't argue with it. Just hang up!

First Corinthians 10:13 promises that God will provide a way of escape. Our task is to find the way and take it. If you don't immediately see the way God has provided, ask Him to reveal it. Fighting starts by putting God in His rightful place in your life. That way, you can lean on Scripture when the devil comes to you with temptation. You can quote the Word of God just like Jesus did when tempted.

There are times I just don't feel like praying or reading the Bible. However, I know I need God's wisdom, which is why every day I read from the books of Psalms and Proverbs. Psalms helps me to better understand how to get along with God, and Proverbs helps me to better understand how to get along with people. The bottom line is I need God's wisdom.

The next time you are tempted or tested, remember this: God will allow temptation in the life of the Christian, but it will always be filtered through the screen of His love. He will always be with you, and He will not allow the temptation to be more than you can stand.

Where Your Strength Comes From

On my way home from the office, I recently stopped to watch a Little League baseball game in the neighborhood. I found a seat on a bench down the first base line and asked one of the boys to update me on the score.

"We're behind 14–0," he said.

I was pleasantly surprised at his upbeat attitude.

"Really? I have to say you don't look very discouraged," I said.

"Discouraged?" the boy responded. "Why should we be discouraged? We haven't been up to bat yet."

Sometimes as Christians, we are going to feel down and depressed, even though we are reading our Bibles, going to church, spending time in prayer with God, and fellowshipping with other believers. Depression creeps in because we are human.

Let's be honest. We all find ourselves in situations where we feel hopeless, helpless, and powerless. But the truth is, you're not hopeless, helpless, or powerless when you have God's Spirit in your life. God says that His mighty power will protect you.

I heard a story during a radio interview with Dr. James Dobson about a letter he had received from a man who was full of bitterness, hatred, and anger. He was so discouraged and depressed that he decided to park his car on the side of a frontage road and then commit suicide by running into the middle of freeway traffic. Fortuitously, the despondent man was also listening to his car radio on the way to his final act. He hit scan on his tuner and it landed on the station where Dobson was delivering his Focus on the Family message. Dobson was telling his audience how much God loves them and how much He wants to forgive them of their sins. And at that moment, the angry, bitter man was done listening to Satan. He was tired of Satan convincing him that he was a loser. In that moment, he asked God to forgive his sins. God showed up through James Dobson's message to protect this man in his weakest moment.

If you will allow Him, God will be there for you as well, and He will place people and resources in your life to help you through times of temptation. God realizes that humans will be tempted by one thing or another in this world. And He cares so deeply about us that He helps guide us through the pitfalls of temptation. Here are some ways He does that:

1. **God draws us close to Himself.** Psalm 34:18 says, "The LORD is close to the brokenhearted and saves those who are crushed in spirit." When we are facing challenges, God may seem a million miles away. But what we feel and what is real are not always the same thing. In fact, God has never been any closer than when we are feeling overwhelmed.

2. **God gives us a church family for support.** We are better together! God intended for us to form communities and to have one another to lean on and offer support. Galatians 6:2 reminds us, "Carry each other's burdens, and in this way you will fulfill the law of Christ." And

Matthew 18:20 says, "For where two or three gather in my name, there am I with them."

3. **God uses temptations to help us grow.** God uses the temptations we face to help us become more like Christ. First, He uses pain or discomfort to get our attention. The Bible says, "Dear brothers and sisters, when troubles of any kind come your way, consider it an opportunity for great joy. For you know that when your faith is tested, your endurance has a chance to grow" (James 1:2–3 NLT). Second, He brings good out of bad (see Romans 8:28). And third, He is preparing us for eternity (see 2 Corinthians 4:17–18).

4. **God gives us the hope of heaven**. If we believe in and trust Jesus Christ for salvation, then we will spend eternity in heaven with God—and that hope will sustain us through every challenge we face. The Bible says, "We do not want you to be uninformed about those who sleep in death, so that you do not grieve like the rest of mankind, who have no hope." (1 Thessalonians 4:13). He promises that all will be set right when we are with Him in eternity.

5. **God uses our pain to help others.** This is called redemptive pain, and it is the highest and best use of our pain. "[God] comforts us in all our troubles, so that we can comfort those in any trouble with the comfort we ourselves receive from God" (2 Corinthians 1:4). Just as Jesus subjected Himself to forty days of trials and temptation by Satan so He could know what we face, God uses our pain and struggle to put us in a place of being able to serve and comfort others when they go through similar situations.

Before Scott's death, guitarist Joe Walsh of the Eagles spoke to him on the telephone, offering him encouragement in his sobriety.

Joe has openly shared that his higher power for two decades was vodka and cocaine. Then he went to rehab in 1994 and has now been sober over twenty-five years. Joe made himself available to visit with Scott and later gave financial gifts for our sober living home. It is selflessness like this that helps us get past our own troubles and temptations to contribute to the greater good.

"Cast out the temptation to move from loneliness to self-pity. Use your lonely feelings to push you toward someone lonelier than you are. The God who blesses you will make you a blessing!" — Dr. David Jeremiah

---

If you are finding temptation too hard to resist, find someone who has greater needs than you do, and then do something to help them. When you've done that, repeat that kindness nine more times.

After Scott's passing, we took comfort in Scripture. We leaned on our church and our friends. In the days and weeks following his death, we received invaluable counsel from pastors Jamie Rasmussen and Rick Warren. They filled our ears and our hearts with words of comfort, underscoring how important it is to have a spiritual infrastructure like the one listed above.

If you know the Lord when you die, you're not leaving home, you're going home! You're going where you were meant to be for all eternity, to "the kingdom [God] prepared for you since the creation of the world" (Matthew 25:34).

Some days I messed up being Scott's dad. Some days I didn't show grace. But every day I loved Scott. Nancy and I do not dwell on the tough years we had as parents with his addiction; instead we reflect on the many good times throughout the years we had with Scott, who was a gift from God. The first person I want to hug when I go to heaven because of God's grace is Jesus, and then my second big hug will be with Scott. I can't wait to see my son again.

Nothing changes lives like the Bible. People struggling with addiction find sobriety, the broken find healing, the hopeless find hope in the Word of God. His Word turns self-centered people into selfless servants, misers into givers, rebels into worshipers, and sinners into saints.

We live daily with problems in our lives, but God gives us strength to persevere. He will give you the power to keep working on the marriage that seems hopeless. He will give you the power to pick yourself up when you've fallen into financial hardship. He'll give you the power to keep your convictions when all the pressure around you says to give in. The key to faith is to be persistent. Keep your eyes on God, not on your problem, because problems are temporary. They won't last forever.

I am tempted every day to do things my way and resist the will of God, which might be the greatest temptation the devil wants to trap us in. Getting us out of the will of God is where he can have his greatest success.

"By the will of God, I will be able to come to you with a joyful heart, and we will be an encouragement to each other." — Romans 15:32 NLT

But there is *joy* in the will of God, and we should not only want to know the will of God but also be anxious to do the will of God every moment of the day. The psalmist David wrote, "I take joy in doing your will, my God, for your instructions are written on my heart" (Psalm 40:8 NLT).

Knowing God's will because it is written on our hearts—it is the Scripture we can quote when we faced temptation—is where we will find our greatest strength to endure the uphill battles that are part of walking in faith.

The late actor Matthew Perry said, "When I die, I don't want *Friends* to be the first thing that's mentioned, since I want to be remembered more importantly for fighting addiction. I'm a drug addict. My life is if I have a drink, I can't stop."[12]

Here is the truth. Having no friends is better than having the wrong friends. You need to be careful if you are hanging around the wrong people. What you need is a friend

. . . who will point you to God;

. . . who's an extension to God (not a substitute for Him);

. . . who will encourage you to draw on the strength of God's promise, especially when you are lonely, having problems, discouraged, or feel like a loser because of your past;

. . . and who will remind you that we can do all things through Christ in His strength (Philippians 4:13).

Finally, remember that God loves you and He is able to do exceedingly abundantly above all that you are asking for your life (Ephesians 3:20). Trust Him!

SCRIPTURE FOR FACING ADDICTION

The Bible compares our Christian life to a running course. We are to "run in such a way" that we'll...

———

... obtain the prize (1 Corinthians 9:24),

———

... "run with endurance" (Hebrews 12:1 NLT),

———

... run without stumbling (Proverbs 4:12),

———

... "run and not be weary" (Isaiah 40:31 NLT),

———

... and finish our course (2 Timothy 4:7).

———

"He is able to help those who are being tempted." (Hebrews 2:18)

———

"The righteous person may have many troubles, but the LORD delivers him from them all." (Psalm 34:19)

———

"We are not trying to please people but God, who tests our hearts." (1 Thessalonians 2:4)

MY FINAL FOUR

*T*he NCAA basketball tournament has come to be known as "March Madness." It is a very popular few weeks of competition building toward the Final Four and the championship game. Because of the impact basketball has made on my life, I have what I call My Final Four. These are the men, among many, who have most influenced my Christian life. These are my spiritual mentors:

Larry Wright

Jerry Colangelo

Rick Warren

Jamie Rasmussen

Even superstars need coaches. The top singers in the world have voice coaches, the top Olympic athletes have trainers, and the top CEOs have business advisers. Coaches help you maximize your strengths and minimize your weaknesses.

This principle of coaching or mentorship is found throughout the Bible. Moses mentored Joshua. Samuel counseled David. David guided Solomon. Elijah coached Elisha.

The apostle Paul also mentored and coached Timothy and many other people. As Paul wrote in 2 Timothy 2:2, "You must teach others those things you and many others have heard me speak about. Teach these great truths to trustworthy men who will, in turn, pass them on to others" (TLB). In mentoring Timothy, Paul expected him to go and instruct faithful men, who would then mentor and coach other faithful men.

God expects the same of faithful men and women today because that's how we grow in discipleship. In fact, I am benefiting right now from the spiritual coaches who have mentored me over my lifetime and helped me grow in different areas of life.

What is a mentor? He or she is a spiritually mature friend and accountability partner who gets real with you and points out sin and weakness while also encouraging your strengths and growth. They help you stay on the path of God's purpose for you.

If you're serious about making the most of your life, then you need to get a coach or mentor to help you fulfill your purpose. They don't have to be perfect. They only have to be one step ahead of you. And, as you grow spiritually, you can be a mentor to someone else!

Now, here are My Final Four.

LARRY WRIGHT

There is no one more responsible for drawing my attention to the Bible than my good friend Larry Wright, who is now home with the Lord.

As I wrote about in the introduction to this book, in 1976 Larry led the first Bible study I ever attended (reluctantly). Even though I liked Larry personally—at the time he was a well-known radio broadcaster at KTAR In Phoenix—I wanted no part of going to a religious Bible study. After all, I went to church most Sundays already and thought that was heavy enough.

My wife, Nancy, had other ideas; she knew I personally needed the Bible study and that it would be good for our marriage if we attended Larry's weekly study together.

I finally gave in to Nancy and said I would go. Looking back, it was without question the best decision I have ever made (and it led to my leading a Bible study in our home).

Before Larry did radio news, he was the most popular disc jockey at KRUX, playing popular music in Phoenix in his earlier years. Larry repeatedly told those who attended his Bible study that when he was in his twenties and thirties he was a real mess, doing everything wrong in his marriage, gambling, staying out late, partying hard, sometimes not coming home because he'd had too much to drink, forgetting his wife on her birthdays and at Christmastime . . . and so on.

Larry would be the first to say his life at that time was a train wreck. His wife, Sue, had two options: to either divorce Larry or to pray for him and love him to the Lord. She decided to pray for Larry and love him like she'd never loved him before, even though he was screwing up everything in his life and in their marriage.

Larry came to the conclusion, "If my wife can love a selfish idiot like me, then God and His love must be real," and that's when Larry's life began to change. Within a short time after Larry received Jesus as his Lord and Savior, he started leading Bible studies in homes and at several country clubs in Phoenix with successful businesspeople.

I remember when I was in Larry's Sunday school class at church, and more than once he told the story that he and Sue, along with their three daughters, would be leaving home headed for church in their car when they would start fighting and arguing all the way there, just before Larry would be teaching Sunday school.

Larry said as soon as his family would reach the church property they would be meeting people at church with big smiles and saying, "Praise the Lord! Praise the Lord!" Then Larry would go to his Bible study room and teach to about one hundred people. As soon as he and his wife and kids got back in the car, they would start fighting and arguing again all the way home.

Larry was real and very transparent in talking about his weaknesses; there was nothing phony about Larry as a Christian. His teaching was biblically based, and he had an amazing sense of humor that made coming to his Sunday school class very fun.

Larry liked to say, "If God said it, I believe it, and that settles it. If He said it, quit arguing with Him. If you don't feel like reading the Bible, then read it anyway."

He also reminded me not to procrastinate when it came to memorizing Scripture. "Watch how God blesses your life when you apply His words," he would tell me.

I thank God for Larry Wright being in my life, and I look forward to being with him again in heaven.

JERRY COLANGELO

I am flawed and imperfect, capable of messing up something every day of the week. That's why I try to surround myself with good people.

I found one of the best when I met Jerry Colangelo.

Jerry relocated his family from Chicago to Phoenix in 1967. He was hired to run the Phoenix Suns, a start-up franchise that joined the NBA in 1968. I met him three weeks after he arrived in the Valley, and our families have been extremely close ever since.

Jerry reached the pinnacle of his profession. He's been a general manager, head coach, and owner of the Suns. He founded the Arizona Diamondbacks in Major League Baseball, and in only their fourth season in the majors, the Diamondbacks under Jerry's leadership won the World Series in 2001 against the New York Yankees. He guided Team USA to four consecutive basketball gold medals. His name is on the court at the Naismith Memorial Basketball Hall of Fame.

But Jerry never let success go to his head. He's never lost sight of his roots or lost focus on what's truly important in life.

Jerry has mentored and coached me during our relationship. I have always admired how he models and prioritizes his life on three important pillars: his faith in God, his love of family, and how much he gives back to the community.

Jesus said, "Let your light shine before others, that they may see your good deeds and glorify your Father in heaven" (Matthew 5:16).

In the Bible, Moses coached Joshua; Samuel coached David, the great king of Israel; and David coached Solomon, the wisest and richest man in the world. In the world of sports, Butch Harmon coached Tiger Woods, the greatest golfer in history. Even Michael Jordan would tell you he often needed a guiding hand, from Dean Smith in college to Phil Jackson in the NBA.

And I believe Jerry Colangelo is as good of a coach as you will find on this planet.

RICK WARREN

Someone gave me Rick Warren's book *The Purpose Driven Life* over twenty years ago. Today it has sold over fifty million copies and has been translated into 137 languages. Rick had no idea that God would use this book to reach and help so many people. *Time* magazine listed Rick as one of the most influential people in the world. To date I have probably purchased and given away almost one thousand copies to many of the friends and acquaintances I have accumulated throughout the years.

I always wanted to meet Rick, and that happened on February 27, 2020, when Jerry Colangelo and I hosted a luncheon at the Arizona Biltmore in Phoenix and Rick was our featured speaker. Rick spoke on "Hope in Tough Times," following Grammy winner

Michael W. Smith singing several songs before approximately five hundred attendees.

When I met Rick at the airport for the first time, we exchanged big hugs. Rick knew that my wife, Nancy, and I had lost our son, Scott, to an accidental overdose on December 12, 2019. Rick understood the pain and suffering Nancy and I were experiencing since he had lost his twenty-seven-year-old son Matthew a few years prior when he took his life after a long battle with mental illness.

Rick spent time ministering to us, which brought us that much closer. He shared the importance of grieving, which is our expression of love for someone we greatly miss, like we do with Scott.

Every day I read Rick's daily newsletter, and each morning I read his daily devotions in his book called *Open Doors*. In addition, I'm privileged that Rick and I from time to time exchange encouraging emails, and that has been very meaningful to me.

If I were to summarize Rick Warren I'd have to say he is "the real deal." As much as any human being, he has helped me with my Christian growth and has become a good friend, which is an enormous blessing!

JAMIE RASMUSSEN

I am blessed today to be under the Bible teaching of Jamie Rasmussen, who is the senior pastor at Scottsdale Bible Church (SBC).

Under Jamie's leadership, SBC has more than seventy-five hundred attendees at four weekly worship services. I benefit from receiving Jamie's weekly teaching because he applies the scriptures in the Bible, which I need to apply in my life.

Jamie is certainly a Bible scholar, but he's also not afraid to tell the large crowds in our church about his own weaknesses. I can relate very well to him, especially when he starts talking about being weak and in need of God's grace and guidance. Jamie's honesty and humility, along with his amazing sense of humor, help me to get real in my life and to pray about my own insecurities and weaknesses.

We know that Jesus was the best storyteller, although I have told Jamie more than once that he's somewhere on the list of great storytellers. He always seems to weave in stories that fit his sermons excellently. Jamie is extremely well prepared when he gives his messages, and his leadership style is both visionary and strategic.

Jamie will keep you on the edge of your seat. He can pivot from talking about Jesus being 100 percent God and 100 percent man when He was God living on earth and went to the cross for us because of His love for a sinner like me . . . to talking about what's wrong with the Browns and why they keep losing (Jamie grew up in Cleveland) . . . to the problems he had with his dad growing up . . . to a funny story about his wife, Kim, needing to correct him on something he did wrong.

In short, Jamie is very down-to-earth; he's a mature Christian who gets the Scriptures right, who consistently emphasizes the importance of the cross, and who never hesitates to tell those in church about the struggles in his own life. Like Rick Warren, he is the "real deal" as he teaches God's Word from the Bible. That's why he always has my attention with his sermons.

Most important, though, Jamie loves God—and in every message he shares, he always leads us to the solution: trust Jesus.

Strength and Wisdom in Common

My Final Four share many positive attributes. At their core, they are men of deep faith who trust and depend on God and His Word.

Rick Warren's ministry is very similar to that of my pastor, Jamie Rasmussen. Plus, Rick's teaching is very much like that of my first mentor, Larry Wright, since all of them are very real with their Bible teaching. I might add the three of them (and

Jerry) have an amazing sense of humor, which certainly keeps my attention.

What do I mean by them being very real as Christians? Rick, Larry, Jerry, and Jamie will be the first to tell you that they are all flawed and have weaknesses; however, they are also very quick to tell you they turn to Jesus for strength and wisdom.

I have discovered through being a believer of Jesus Christ that there are believers who are very real and draw people to Christ by their lifestyle. But also, at the risk of sounding judgmental, it's really pretty easy to find a fake Christian who isn't real and appears as phony as a three-dollar bill.

I thank God for blessing me with such authentic mentors and friends.

CONCLUSION

THE PATH TO GREATNESS

Walking by Faith, Serving in Love has been written to encourage and challenge all of us to think about the legacy we are building. I pray you will be blessed by this book, which has many scriptures and stories I hope you will find meaningful.

Stories, after all, are not the icing on the cake; they are the cake! The Bible is filled with stories, and when Jesus wanted to get someone's attention He almost always told a story. Purposeful storytelling can motivate, win over, shape, engage, and change lives. I believe the marketplace wants and needs stories, and I have set out to provide them here.

In writing this book I also want to lead from my heart, not my head. Heroes come in all shapes and sizes, but a giving heart tends to unite them all.

My experience is that when I label someone a *hero* I find their path of greatness is the humility in their life and their willingness to serve and help others.

I know better than anyone my imperfections, weaknesses, and insecurities. Whenever I tell my story, I want to be transparent and real, and I hope that has come through in these pages.

I have also discovered the importance of being vulnerable, which is not a liability but an asset. I am still flawed in so many ways, even though I have been a Christian for many years and have led Bible studies for five decades.

I believe theologian and author C. S. Lewis was spot-on when said the Bible is not designed to increase our knowledge, but to change our life. God's Word has indeed changed my life, I am so much the better for it, and I know that the Bible (and, most important, the Author of the book, who is the living Word) can and will transform your life and your destiny as well.

A NOTE FROM WRITER
DAN BICKLEY

$\mathcal{J}$immy wanted the following message to come from him before I write about the Jimmy Walker that I know:

Writer Dan Bickley

I know I am flawed as a human and as a Christian. In many ways I am broken and inadequate. I know I am imperfect. Aside from Christ I am insecure. The biggest room in the world is the room for improvement. I know I can improve, and I have learned so much in the many years of my life.

Michelangelo was asked at age eighty-six when he was going to retire and he replied, "When I quit learning." I believe I have learned more in life from my failures than my successes. Without Christ in my life, I know how to envy other people; I know how to feel sorry for myself; I know how to judge when I shouldn't be judging. I know how to have a pity party when things don't go my way.

Paul, who wrote the majority of the New Testament, said we are all sinners and that he was the biggest sinner of all. I've known the Lord for many years, and I know that I am still a work in progress.

"He who began a good work in you will carry it on to completion" (Philippians 1:6). I interpret this scripture to mean God is not finished with me yet. I am thankful for God's grace.

I know there are many people who go unnoticed who do many more good things than I do when it comes to serving and helping other people.

Jimmy makes it clear that his priorities in his life are faith, family, business, and friends. I want to touch on the subjects absorbing much of Jimmy's time—his service to others in need—which he considers very important as a Christian.

"To whom much is given, much is expected" (see Luke 12:48). I believe this scripture helps to describe Jimmy Walker, since he has an amazing passion to serve.

But don't just take it from me. Lionel Richie said, "What Jimmy continues to do for charity is amazing. I don't know where he has the time to do what he does. Jimmy is God's messenger on steroids. How can one man have so many projects on his plate and still have time for his own life? The answer: Passion."

And Billy Crystal said, "Jimmy Walker is a walking angel . . . one of those people who doesn't know how to do anything else but to help people."

Here are just some of the many ways Jimmy has worked tirelessly to live up to that reputation:

- Jimmy organized twenty-seven Celebrity Fight Night Charity Events in Phoenix, giving approximately $100 million to charity. He started it in 1994 with Charles Barkley when Jimmy was a limited partner in the Phoenix Suns, and then Muhammad Ali co-led this charity event with Jimmy for twenty years before he passed. The lead beneficiary was the Muhammad Ali Parkinson Center at the Barrow Neurological Institute, where Jimmy has been a board member.

- Jimmy has organized six charity events in Italy with the Andrea Bocelli Foundation, raising $18 million for charity. Performances by entertainers (in addition to Andrea Bocelli) have included Elton John, Steven Tyler, Reba McEntire, David Foster, Lionel Richie, John Legend, and many more. Among the well-known people honored in Italy at the charity event have been Sophia Loren and George Clooney.

- In 1983, Jimmy and his family started a Bicycle Party for inner-city children during the Christmas season. This annual event has been supported by many friends of the Walker family for over forty years. To date, approximately ten thousand bicycles have been given to these young kids, some of whom are homeless or living in shelters—so a brand-new bike is beyond their imagining.

- For almost twelve years, from March 28, 2008, until February 17, 2020, every Monday morning at 7:00 a.m., Jimmy arranged for businesspeople, celebrities, and other influencers to speak to about five hundred homeless men and women during breakfast. The program was called Never Give Up and featured approximately 450 guest speakers throughout the years, offering inspiration and insight for people struggling to survive. Jimmy would open with a brief, encouraging message for the homeless to *never give up*. The first speaker was the late Hall of Fame basketball player Bob Lanier.

- Jimmy invited some fifteen Christians with a platform to give their testimonies in the Walkers' backyard in Phoenix for about two hundred people when he and his wife, Nancy, hosted dinner parties during the 1980s.

- Jimmy organized a large steak dinner over four years cooked by four of Phoenix's best chefs for five hundred homeless men and women at St. Vincent de Paul, serving lunch every year on January 17 to honor Muhammad Ali on his birthday. The event was sponsored by some of Jimmy's friends.

- Jimmy arranged for Andrea Bocelli to sing at 7:00 a.m. in 40° weather in 2014 to about two hundred homeless men and women at St. Vincent de Paul. Andrea sang "Ave Maria" on the basketball court, which Celebrity Fight Night had donated.

- Jimmy organized two charity events at Brush Creek Ranch in Wyoming with Reba McEntire. They raised $5 million for charity.

- Jimmy spearheaded an event to honor Jerry Colangelo, chairman of Team USA basketball, when he brought home the gold from the 2008 Beijing Olympics. Some six hundred people attended the celebration at the Arizona Biltmore in Phoenix.

- Jimmy organized a charity luncheon to honor Reggie Jackson, with two hundred guests, at the Sanctuary Resort in Scottsdale during the 2011 MLB All-Star game.

- For most of the years between 1978 and 2019, Jimmy led a Bible study for groups ranging from ten to sixty people. He led the majority of these studies in hotels and restaurants or at his home.

- From 2020 to the time of this writing, Jimmy has led a Wednesday Night Speakers' program for about twenty men recovering from drug and alcohol addiction at the Walkers' nonprofit Sober Living Home called Scott's Place.

- Jimmy, along with his friend Jerry Colangelo, present a faith-based broadcast several times each year with Christians sharing their testimonies that is circulated on social media. In addition, Jimmy and Jerry organized a large luncheon in 2020 in Phoenix with about five hundred people in which Rick Warren spoke and Grammy winner Michael W. Smith sang.
- Jimmy organized the Jerry Colangelo Appreciation Luncheon at the Arizona Biltmore on October 4, 2023, where five hundred attendees honored the former owner of the Phoenix Suns and Arizona Diamondbacks.
- On April 20, 2024, Jimmy organized a complimentary dinner for 550 men and women who are recovering from drugs and alcohol, some of whom shared encouraging testimonies. Sixteen-time Grammy winner David Foster and his wife, Katherine, entertained, along with Pia Toscano and Daniel Emmet.

While this list is lengthy and represents an incalculable impact, it is far from the whole story of Jimmy's inspiring influence. Nor is he slowing down. As you will read in the following pages, Jimmy continues in his unshakable commitment to honor all that God has given to him, to share the love of Jesus with everyone he meets, and to proclaim the power of walking by faith and serving in love. Jimmy says, "I am not retiring, I'm refiring!"

Enjoy!

ACKNOWLEDGMENTS

I want to thank the pastors and Christian leaders below who have assisted me with this book and with the life of faith. These men and women have helped my Christian growth:

Ken Blanchard

Mark Buckley

Dr. David Jeremiah

Greg Laurie

Anne Graham Lotz

John MacArthur

John Maxwell

Jamie Rasmussen

Adrian Rogers

Charles Stanley

Rick Warren

Michael Youssef

INDEX

ENDNOTES

Chapter 6 – Why I Find It Difficult to Forgive
1   Rick Warren, *Open Doors: A Year of Daily Devotions* (Lake Forest, CA: Purpose Driven Publishing, 2019).

Chapter 12 – Why I Want to Be Successful
2   *Affluenza*, PBS (1997), https://www.pbs.org/kcts/affluenza/.
3   Julia Gomez, "2024 World Happiness Report: Happiest Countries Revealed US Fails to Crack Top 20," *USA Today*, March 20, 2024, https://www.usatoday.com/story/news/world/2024/03/20/2024-world-happiness-report-rankings/73039460007/.

Chapter 14 — Why I Can Be Influenced by the World
4   Dr. George Barna, "American Worldview Inventory 2024," Cultural Research Center at Arizona Christian University, April 23, 2024, https://www.arizonacristian.edu/wp-content/uploads/2024/04/CRC-Release-AWVI-2-April-23-2024.pdf.
5   "Kevin 27 years BK," GoFundMe, https://www.gofundme.com/f/kevin-27-years.

Chapter 15: Why I Care about the Poor
6   "Howard Schultz, Real Time Net Worth," *Forbes*, accessed May 1, 2024, https://www.forbes.com/profile/howard-schultz/?sh=1d0dc4d652c6.
7   "John Paul DeJoria, Real Time Net Worth," *Forbes*, accessed May 1, 2024, https://www.forbes.com/profile/john-paul-dejoria/?sh=560031c824a4.

Chapter 16: Why I Want to Help People to Be Sober
8   Movieguide Staff, "Alice Cooper: People Avoid Believing in Jesus Because They 'Don't Want to Give Up Their Godship,'" Movieguide, September 30, 2021, https://www.movieguide.org/news-articles/alice-cooper-people-avoid-believing-in-jesus-because-they-dont-want-to-give-up-their-godship.html.

9   "Why Are So Many Kids and Teens Cutting?" Amen Clinics, March 17, 2021, https://www.amenclinics.com/blog/why-are-so-many-kids-and-teens-cutting/.

10   Matthew F. Garnett, MPH, Sally C. Curtin, MA, and Deborah M. Stone, ScD, "Suicide Mortality in the United States, 2000-2020," *CDC Data Briefs* 433, (March 2022), https://www.cdc.gov/nchs/products/databriefs/db433.htm#:~: text=The%20overall%20suicide%20rate%20increased,2018%20and%20 2020%20to%2013.5.

11   "DEA Laboratory Testing Reveals that 6 out of 10 Fentanyl-Laced Fake Prescription Pills Now Contain a Potentially Lethal Dose of Fentanyl," United States Drug Enforcement Administration, https://www.dea.gov/alert/dea-laboratory-testing-reveals-6-out-10-fentanyl-laced-fake-prescription-pills-now-contain.

12   Carson Blackwelder, "How Matthew Perry Said He Wanted to Be Remembered Beyond 'Friends,'" *ABC News*, October 30, 2023, https://abcnews.go.com/ GMA/Culture/matthew-perry-wanted-remembered-beyond-friends/ story?id=104474000.